Choosing

Your

Faith

CHOOSING YOUR FAITH

In a World of Spiritual Options

FOREWORD BY **LEE STROBEL**

MARK MITTELBERG

WILLOW
Willow Creek Resources

TYNDALE HOUSE PUBLISHERS, INC., CAROL STREAM, ILLINOIS

Visit Tyndale's exciting Web site at www.tyndale.com

TYNDALE and Tyndale's quill logo are registered trademarks of Tyndale House Publishers, Inc.

Choosing Your Faith . . . In a World of Spiritual Options

Copyright © 2008 by Mark Mittelberg. All rights reserved.

Cover photo of door copyright © by Svilen Milev/Stock Xchange. All rights reserved.

Cover photo of doorknob copyright © by Tony Colter/iStockphoto. All rights reserved.

Author photo copyright © by Gary Payne. All rights reserved.

Designed by Stephen Vosloo and Julie Chen

Edited by Dave Lindstedt

Published in association with the literary agency of Alive Communications, Inc.,
7680 Goddard Street, Suite 200, Colorado Springs, CO 80920.

Unless otherwise indicated, all Scripture quotations are taken from *The Holy Bible*,
New Living Translation, copyright © 1996, 2004. Used by permission of Tyndale House
Publishers, Inc., Carol Stream, Illinois 60188. All rights reserved.

Scripture quotations marked NIV are taken from the HOLY BIBLE, NEW INTERNATIONAL
VERSION®. NIV®. Copyright © 1973, 1978, 1984 by International Bible Society. Used by
permission of Zondervan. All rights reserved.

Scripture quotations marked KJV are taken from *The Holy Bible*, King James Version.

Library of Congress Cataloging-in-Publication Data

Mittelberg, Mark.
    Choosing your faith : in a world of spiritual options / Mark Mittelberg ; foreword by Lee
Strobel.
        p. cm.
    Includes bibliographical references.
    ISBN-13: 978-1-4143-1579-9 (hc)
    ISBN-10: 1-4143-1579-1 (hc)
    1. Apologetics.   2. Choice (Psychology)—Religious aspects—Christianity.   I. Title.
BT1103.M58 2008
239—dc22   2007045075

Printed in the United States of America

14   13   12   11   10   09   08

7   6   5   4   3   2   1

To my wonderful parents,
Orland and Virginia Mittelberg,
who patiently provided spiritual guidance,
but graciously allowed me to
choose my faith.

CONTENTS

FOREWORD

by Lee Strobel, author of The Case for Faith

I wish this book had been available on January 20, 1980.

That's the day I decided to reevaluate my atheism and consider whether there was any convincing evidence to believe in God—*any* God, whether the God of Islam, Christianity, Mormonism, Judaism, or even the multiplicity of gods in Hinduism. Impressed by my wife's transformation since she had become a Christian, I vowed to use my training in journalism and law (I was the legal-affairs editor of the *Chicago Tribune*) to launch a full-fledged investigation of spiritual matters.

My quest would have been considerably easier if I'd had this invaluable guide at the time. As Mark Mittelberg brilliantly describes, all of us take different pathways in our journeys of spiritual discovery. Whether we realize it or not, we're influenced by a myriad of factors, some of which can take us toward the truth, while others simply lead us into confusion. These insights would have been extremely helpful as I tried to sort through the competing spiritual beliefs on my own.

You're fortunate—if you're a spiritual seeker, you've now got this terrific guidebook to help you maneuver through the minefield of conflicting and contradictory claims about spirituality. You'll find Mark to be a thoughtful, empathetic, and discerning friend as you go through this eye-opening and heart-expanding process together.

But this book isn't intended only for seekers. Christians also will discover their own spiritual style, which will serve to bolster their beliefs, while at the same time helping them to better understand how they can assist their friends as they seek a faith that makes sense.

I can't think of anyone who is better positioned than Mark to serve as your spiritual coach. Yes, he has excellent academic credentials, having earned a graduate degree in philosophy of religion. But beyond that, Mark has spent the last two decades helping everyday people figure out how to choose their faith. He lives in the trenches of real life, not in some distant ivory tower.

You'll find that Mark isn't going to preach at you. He gives due consideration to various approaches to the spiritual realm. His style in this book is to walk alongside you as you weigh the spiritual options and come to your own conclusions about where the evidence convincingly points.

Having been Mark's friend and ministry partner for twenty years, I can attest to his sterling character, his godly lifestyle, and his heartfelt desire to assist others as they seek the truth about spiritual topics. Does he have his own convictions about God? You bet. But he's not going to try to unilaterally impose them on you. Instead, he wants to befriend you as you embark on the most exciting and stimulating journey of your life, discovering for yourself where the truth really resides.

Every Monday, Mark and I get together for lunch. It's one of the highlights of my week because I'm constantly learning something new from him. We talk about the mundane and the lofty, but we frequently circle back to discussing how we can know for sure that our spiritual beliefs are well-placed. One thing amazes me: Mark's deep reservoir of wisdom never runs dry.

So pull up a chair and join us. Wherever you are in your spiritual adventure, you're going to find yourself encouraged and challenged. But most of all, you're going to walk away with everything you need to make the most important faith decisions of your life.

ACKNOWLEDGMENTS

I would never have been able to complete this book about choosing a faith path without first having been the recipient of the faith, support, encouragement, and prayers of the following people:

Lee Strobel, my close friend and ministry partner of twenty years, who spurred me on and helped me move forward from the inception to the completion of this project. He said it well when he once wrote, "We're each other's biggest boosters. I have more confidence in Mark than he has in himself, and that's how he feels about me. That makes for a terrific combination!" It was my turn to be on the receiving end of that encouragement, and I am deeply grateful.

To Heidi, my incredibly supportive and patient wife, and our two great teenage kids, Emma Jean and Matthew—thanks for the prayers and cheers, not to mention coffee and snacks at odd times of the day and night, frequent ping-pong matches, and occasional breaks for ice cream or walks around the lake with our little pal Charlie (the Cavalier).

Thanks to Dr. Chad Meister for your philosophical wisdom and editorial input. Your generous sharing of knowledge and insights served me and the readers of this book immeasurably. Thanks, too, to Brad Mitchell, for reading the manuscript and providing feedback, as well as for providing spiritual "air support." Tom Chapin and Nabeel Qureshi also gave important feedback at critical points.

Appreciation to Don Pape, who helped get the ball rolling, and to Beth Jusino at Alive Communications, who helped keep it on track and who provided shots of encouragement along the way. I'm also indebted to my philosophical mentors, the late Bob Passantino and his wife Gretchen, William Lane Craig, Norman Geisler, and especially Stuart Hackett—including the early influence of a dusty old textbook Dr. Hackett assigned to his students: *The Ways of Knowing* by William Montague.

Thanks, as well, for the partnering efforts and encouragement of Scott and Susan Evans, Ron Forseth, Jennifer Dion, Eric Abel, Lynne Marian, Chad Cannon, Kim Levings, and all my friends at Outreach, Inc. Also, the support of Paul Braoudakis of the Willow Creek Association, Bill Dallas and Jay Mitchell of CCN, as well as the prayers and encouragement of Chris and Carla Wilson, Karl and Barbara Singer, Kevin and Sherry Harney, Nancy Grisham, Terry Schulenburg, Mike Licona, Hillis and Jean Hugelen, and Orland and Ginny Mittelberg.

Last, but certainly not least, a special thanks to Jon Farrar, Ron Beers, and the team at Tyndale House Publishers for believing in me. Also, to my editor, Dave Lindstedt, for making sure my words made sense, as well as to Maria Eriksen, Charlie Swaney, and their great teams for getting the word out about this book.

To all of you—and to any I failed to mention—I offer my sincere thanks.

CHAPTER ONE

"WHY CHOOSE *ANY* FAITH?"

"Choose a faith"? Why would anyone even want one?

Faith sounds dangerously close to *religion*—and the rock band R.E.M. pretty well expressed the feelings of a generation when they released their infectious anthem "Losing My Religion." Never mind whether anybody, including me, ever really understood what the song was about. Michael Stipe, the guy who wrote and sang the lyrics, said in an interview that the phrase "losing my religion" is actually a figure of speech that means "coming to the end of your rope." "And," he added, "it's a secular song and has little or nothing to do with religion."[1]

But that hasn't stopped countless people from singing their hearts out whenever the song plays on the radio:

THAT'S ME IN THE CORNER
THAT'S ME IN THE SPOTLIGHT
I'M LOSING MY RELIGION
TRYING TO KEEP UP WITH YOU[2]

I looked up the song on YouTube.com and read the comments people had written about it. Even now, roughly two decades after the song was first released, people are still trying to figure it out:

ANIMEMMA (3 MONTHS AGO)
   THIS IS A GOOD SONG B/C RELIGION IS FALSE
NAKASII00 (3 MONTHS AGO)
   ANIMEMMA, LOSING MY RELIGION IS SOUTHERN SLANG FOR
   BEING FED UP, IDIOT

Not that there aren't plenty of reasons, with or without R.E.M.'s song, to feel ambivalent about—or even negative toward—the realm of religion. Most of us have at least a few reasons of our own. Mine, admittedly, are not all that weighty.

For me, it's the memory of having to get up every Sunday, earlier than it seemed any kid should have to on a weekend, and rushing around trying to get ready, putting on what my family called "Sunday clothes." These were articles of apparel I'd never think of wearing any other day of the week. They were usually too small, or too large ("It's okay," my dad would say. "You'll grow into them."); out of style (as if they were ever *in* style); and often itchy. Sometimes, my parents even made me wear a sport coat and tie! I'm pretty sure that today, particularly where I live in Southern California, the Department of Children and Family Services would take kids out of a home for that kind of abuse—especially when the top button on my shirt was always too tight and would choke me whenever I tried to breathe. Occasionally, even now, thinking about going to church can give me a pinching sensation in the front of my throat.

Almost without exception, after finally getting ready, I'd bound down the stairs to find the house empty. But that didn't mean I was off the hook. It meant I had to run out to the street to discover that my family was already in the car, waiting impatiently for me.

"Hurry up, Mark, we're running late again!"

By the time we got to church, I'd be so out of sorts that it was really hard to think about lofty things like God or serious spiritual stuff.

Later, when I was in junior high and then in high school, I became increasingly aware of how strange most church music was. The organ produced notes that were eerily similar to the sounds I'd heard in low-budget haunted-house movies. In fact, most of the traditional church songs (*hymns*, to use the proper word) were written by people from another era, apparently *for* the people from another era—people who liked to sit in pews and sing hymns before going to hang out with their friends in the church "narthex" or "vestibule." I remember one service in which none of the nine songs played had been written within the past one hundred years—and some dated back several centuries. Nothing against relics or antiques, but it struck me that there was something anachronistic and culturally out-of-sync about much of what I was experiencing in my religious environment.

Increasingly, I came to view my life in two categories: normal and religious. *Normal* related to everyday, ordinary life, like school, spending time with my friends, and having fun. *Religious* related to weighty things like faith, beliefs, teachings about right and wrong—and a Sunday experience with nice (often overly nice) people, who meant well but sometimes seemed to come from a planet far from the world I lived in. And that world—the normal one—was the one that was becoming more and more exciting to me, while the religious one was becoming . . . well, increasingly distant and boring. I reached the point where I was rapidly losing interest in all things spiritual and wanted to minimize my exposure to religion in general.

It struck me that there was something anachronistic and culturally out-of-sync about much of what I was experiencing in my religious environment.

I still had to go to church services during that time, however, so a couple of my renegade friends and I would do whatever we could to make the Sunday experience more bearable. Sometimes, we'd hide out in the furnace room in the church basement until the service was over. We'd sit quietly, listen carefully, and try to time things so that we could nonchalantly emerge and blend into the departing crowd.

Other times, we'd sit through the service, but we'd look for ways to amuse ourselves as the minutes slowly ticked by. For instance, sometimes we'd take turns seeing who could hold his breath the longest. I can only imagine what the people sitting around us must have thought as my friends and I hyperventilated to collect maximum levels of oxygen in our lungs, and then took a huge, time-me-on-this-one breath and held it for as long as we possibly could. A strange way to pass the time, I know—but one fine Sunday morning I did manage to break the three-minute barrier!

∞

As I mentioned, my adolescent problems with religion were trivial compared to those of many other people, perhaps even your own. For some, the issues are really serious, like those of my friend who, as a young man, left his church after experiencing abuse at the hands of religious leaders. These were the very people who should have been nurturing and protecting him, not to mention setting a good example. That was many years ago, but even now he's not showing any interest in ever going back.

Reports of abusive clergy have grown increasingly frequent in recent years. And as awful as they are, I don't know which is worse: the crimes themselves, or the cover-ups at higher levels of leadership—where often those in charge merely reassigned the perpetrators, time and again, to new territories, foisting the offenders upon fresh, unsuspecting parishes.

When it isn't sexual impropriety making the news these days, it seems it's financial corruption. We've certainly seen enough of those stories over the years.

But problems tied to religion are not isolated to Protestants and Catholics. In recent years, the Muslim world has been rocked by horrendous events such as the 9/11 attacks and increasing instances of terrorism around the world. It's to the point where the concepts of "Islam" and "terrorism" have become inseparable in many people's minds. Though this connection may not be fair to many peace-loving Muslims, the perception is a reality that colors the way we all look at the subject of religion, and it may affect whether we'd ever be willing to actually consider choosing a faith of our own.

Add to these examples the many cults and religious groups that stand on street corners or show up uninvited to knock on our doors, as they try to sell us their materials and recruit us into their flocks. University students in particular have to be cautious. There was a time when, with one weak moment, they could find themselves off somewhere at a remote retreat with a bunch of smiling, zombie-like zealots. These people promised them happiness but systematically robbed them of their identity, individuality, and relationships—as well as their dreams for the future. And while these groups' followers gave up everything they had to serve and spread their message, their leaders often indulged in material excess and outright immorality as they privately, and sometimes even publicly, modeled everything that was contrary to the religious piety they claimed to represent. Today, many of those aberrant religious groups have become more subtle in their approach, but they can be every bit as damaging to those they snare.

This hypocrisy and abuse leave such a strong taste in people's mouths that they have helped foster a new movement of authors and influencers who not only reject religion for themselves but teach that all of it—from the bizarre cults to the benign corner congregations—is dangerous and evil for everyone else, too. Examples include books like *The God Delusion* by Richard Dawkins, *The End of Faith* by Sam Harris, and *God Is Not Great: How Religion Poisons Everything* by Christopher

Hitchens. Or consider the words of Rosie O'Donnell, who declared on the national TV show *The View*, "Radical Christianity is just as threatening as radical Islam."

The message is clear: *If you mess around with religion, you do so at your own risk. And if you get too serious about it, the effects can be devastating. So why even mess with it at all?*

But here's what's interesting: Though antireligious sentiment seems to be spreading throughout society, there's a simultaneous resurgence of interest in spiritual matters. Just look at a few examples:

- the growing roster of TV specials and news programs discussing Jesus, the history and background of the Bible, archeological discoveries, claims of the miraculous, and Christianity contrasted to other world religions

- the increasing number of faith-oriented films showing up in local theaters—some of which, like Mel Gibson's *The Passion of the Christ*, have become worldwide blockbusters

- the array of religious themes featured on the covers of newsmagazines, especially around Christmas and Easter, as well as on Internet blogs, podcasts, and Web sites

- the scriptural subjects of some of the songs on the popular music charts, from the once ubiquitous "What If God Was One of Us" to many of the songs by religiously oriented bands such as U2, Creed, P.O.D., Lifehouse, Switchfoot, and The Fray

Apparently, spirituality sells. But it wouldn't sell if it weren't scratching an itch. As it has often been observed, people are, generally speaking, "incurably religious."

The studies and statistics bear this out. A recent Gallup poll found that 94 percent of people in the United States still believe in God or in a universal spirit.[3] In an average week, more people attend American churches than attend all American sporting events combined.[4] And the Bible, even after so much skepticism has been spread about its message and historical validity, continues to be the best-selling book of all time—by a long shot. Karl Marx said that religion is "the opium of the masses." I guess people are having a hard time giving up the addiction.

But at a deeper level, don't you feel the pull yourself? After all the bad raps and beatings that religion has taken in recent years, why is it that so many people are still so interested? And why are you yourself drawn to spirituality enough to be willing to pick up and read—at least this far—a book about faith?

A recent Gallup poll found that 94 percent of people in the United States still believe in God or in a universal spirit.

Why do we so often look at the beauty of a sunset or observe the wonder of childbirth and sense that there has got to be something undergirding all of this at a deeper level?

What is it that makes us aware, at least in our more honest, lying-awake moments, that there really must be more to life than the flurry of activities that keeps our heads spinning but our souls shrinking as we slog along, day after day, year after year? Why is it that we often feel a longing for a truly calm and centered life, one that is more in tune with the transcendent and less caught up in the tumultuous here and now? Where does the guilt that we sometimes grapple with emanate from—and what can we do to alleviate those guilty feelings and the sense of spiritual inadequacy that so often weigh us down?

It's easy to criticize and even write off organized religion with some of its incompetent or even corrupt spiritual leaders and their annoying antics. These targets are obvious and hard not to hit—but focusing on them fails to address the deeper aching of our souls, the inescapable awareness that life as we know it is not as it was intended to be, the knowledge that we need some kind of outside help to really get things right. What do we do with all that?

Maybe you can relate to some of this, but because you're suspicious of *all* faiths, you don't feel ready to hear about how to choose one for yourself. You'd rather wait it out until you can "just know"—rather than put your trust in anything. If that's how you feel, I've got to tell you something that might be a bit surprising and even unsettling: You've already got a "faith," and you're living by trust in that faith daily. Really!

∞

Think about your day so far. This morning, you got up and had breakfast—by faith—trusting that nobody in the house had laced your food with poison. You stopped at a coffee shop and somehow trusted those characters behind the counter (is that really a good idea?) not to put some kind of harmful substance in your triple-shot, extra foam latte. You got to work—maybe even took the elevator?—and sat in a chair, by faith, without testing it first to see if it was still strong enough to hold you.

You started your computer and typed in confidential information, even though you knew that the latest Internet virus could take that information and broadcast it to everyone in your address book. At lunch, you went out for a walk and paused to bend down and pat a stranger's dog, believing you wouldn't become one of the 4.7 million Americans bitten by a dog each year (of whom 1,008 have to go to the emergency room *every day*). Then, at the end of the day, you aimed your car toward home and drove down the street, trusting-but-not-really-knowing that some sixteen-year-old NASCAR wannabe wouldn't be out drag racing his friends, careening toward you at a high rate of speed.

No doubt about it—you live your life by faith every day, even in the mundane details. You may have what seem like good reasons for your faith, which is fine, but you could also be wrong about some of your conclusions. And some of those mistakes could be serious, even life threatening.

More than that, even if you're a thoroughly nonreligious person, you're living with the hope that your nonreligious beliefs are accurate, and that you won't someday face a thoroughly religious Maker who, come to find out, actually did once issue a list of moral requirements, which you routinely failed to pay attention to.

"Oh, I never worry about things like that," you may say. But that statement itself is an expression of faith that it's okay not to concern oneself with such things. You don't *know* that they are unimportant—you just *believe* that to be the case. That's part of your own particular version of nonreligious faith.

Even well-known atheists such as Richard Dawkins and Sam Harris live their lives with an unproven assumption that there is no God and that the opinions they express are ultimately helping and not harming themselves and others. They don't *know* that they are correct—they just *hope* so.

In fact, Dawkins, who is probably the greatest evangelist for atheism of our day, admitted in an interview recorded in *Time* magazine that "there could be something incredibly grand and incomprehensible and beyond our present understanding."

Biochemist Francis Collins, who was arguing the other side in the interview, shot back, "That's God."

Dawkins replied, "Yes. But it could be any of a billion Gods. It could be God of the Martians or of the inhabitants of Alpha Centauri. The chance of its being a particular God, Yahweh, the God of Jesus, is vanishingly small—at the least, the onus is on you to demonstrate why you think that's the case."[5]

Whether the chances are large or small, the important thought to catch here is that *Dawkins doesn't know there is no God*—and he even concedes the possibility that some kind of God might actually exist. Rather, he takes it on *faith* that there actually is no God.

Even if you're a thoroughly nonreligious person, you're living with the hope that your nonreligious beliefs are accurate.

Now, I'm sure he would argue that this is an educated conclusion, supported by the preponderance of evidence. But even if he turned out to be right, it doesn't change the fact that his conclusion is based on faith. In other words, it's a conclusion that seems to him to be the right one, based on the data he has examined—but one that goes beyond what can be proven or known with complete certainty.

That's just the way life is. We *all* live by some form of faith.

Which leads us to the central question: Is ours a well-founded faith? A wise faith? A faith that makes sense and is supported by the facts? One that works in real life and is worth hanging on to?

More personally, is yours a faith you've really thought about, carefully evaluated, and intentionally chosen—or did you just slide into it at some point along the way?

∞

When I got to college, I came to the painful realization that I'd grown into my particular version of faith rather passively. I'd been raised believing in God, trusting in the Bible, and having faith that the church was the carrier of God's truth. And I had an unsubstantiated and naive confidence in the truth of all this.

Then I signed up for some philosophy classes. One of my professors, who was a religious man of a different stripe, seemed to delight in dismantling the simplistic beliefs of many of his Christian students—and I felt like I was a favorite target. He skillfully pointed out problems with the Bible, with what he called "traditional views about God," and with most of the things I'd been taught to believe. His intellectual onslaught woke me up and made me face the fact that I'd bought into a belief system that I barely understood and had never critically analyzed.

I hardly knew how to respond, and I have to admit that my attempts to get better answers from some of the leaders at my church were generally disheartening. For example, I told one of my teachers that my faith was being assailed in school and that I needed a deeper understanding not only of what we believed, but also of why we thought it was correct.

"How do we know that the Bible is really true and that it is actually God's Word?" I asked. I'll never forget his reply: "Oh that's easy, it says right here in the New Testament that 'all scripture is given by inspiration of God, and is profitable for doctrine, for reproof, for correction, for instruction in righteousness.'"

"Yes, but how do we know that what *that* says is true?" I replied.

"Because it says it is," he answered, "and it's God's Word."

"But that's the very question we're trying to answer," I shot back. "If all you do is appeal to the Bible's claims to prove that the Bible is true, then you're guilty of circular reasoning, and you've proved nothing."

When I got to college, I came to the painful realization that I'd grown into my particular version of faith rather passively.

He looked at me like he was certain I was rapidly sinking into the quicksands of liberalism or skepticism—or had already become an actual infidel—and then, with a deep breath, took another run at it: "But you need to realize that there's no higher authority than God's revelation. If God says it's true, then you can bank your life on it."

"Okay," I replied wearily, "but how do you know that God's really the one talking here? Lots of religious books claim to be God talking—and you don't believe those other books."

"*That's because,*" he said triumphantly, "*those other books are not the Word of God!*"

At this point, I was frustrated enough to wish I could imitate Indiana Jones in that scene from *Raiders of the Lost Ark* where he finally gets fed up with his sword-wielding opponent's antics and just pulls out his pistol and shoots the guy. Of course I'm only kidding (at least now I am). But it was becoming abundantly clear to me that logic was not going to get me any further in that conversation, so I finally just had to let it go—although I was left with the same questions churning in my mind.

Subsequently, I found some people and books that were a lot more helpful. I'll come back to my story later, but this exasperating interchange, and others like it along the way, helped me realize that lots of religious people hold firmly to all kinds of religious ideas—whether right or wrong—for all kinds of weak and apparently unfounded, or at least unexamined, reasons. I determined then and there that whether I ended up agreeing with the faith of my upbringing or choosing a completely different point of view, my conclusion would have to be based on more solid criteria than what some of my teachers and leaders were apparently clinging to.

∞

I recently bought a new mountain bike. That may not sound like a big deal to you, but for me it was quite an event. That's because I no longer live in the Midwest where most of my "mountain biking" was really just *biking without any mountains*—or even any serious hills, for that matter. Now I live in the foothills of the Santa Ana Mountains of California, and I knew it was time to finally research and invest in a full suspension, no-nonsense mountain bike. So I subscribed to *Mountain Bike Action* magazine, searched online, and started reading all kinds of reviews and articles.

I knew I wanted a bike that would be lightweight but also extremely durable. So I studied up on the pros and cons of the various options for frame materials, including steel, titanium, aluminum, and carbon fiber. That last option seemed the most unlikely choice, at least at first, because I was planning to go on some serious trails—with big rocks, sharp turns, and plenty of drops and obstacles—and the idea of entrusting my safety to some kind of newfangled synthetic glass or plastic or whatever-it-really-is frame just didn't seem like a good idea.

But I kept reading and researching, doing Google searches on the Internet, and talking to any expert who would take the time to interact with me. Guess what I learned? Carbon fiber is stronger than aluminum or steel and is even lighter than titanium. It's expensive, but it provides a great combination of strength and weight, and it looks good, too.

Lots of religious people hold firmly to all kinds of religious ideas—whether right or wrong—for all kinds of weak and apparently unfounded, or at least unexamined, reasons.

I probably don't need to tell you I ended up buying a carbon-fiber mountain bike. After months of research, I bought the top frame for the money, and I also carefully researched, read reviews, and got expert advice on the best components to build onto the frame, including the fork, rear shock, crank, derailleurs, shifters, brakes (front and rear hydraulic disc brakes, no less), handlebar, stem, seat post, saddle, wheel sets, tires—I even spent a fair amount of time reading up on the best pedals and riding shoes to purchase.

The result is that I now have a bike I love to ride, and it is serving me really well. (Honestly, it's gotta be the coolest bike on the planet. It oughta be—I paid the price of a motorcycle, but got a cycle without the motor. Worse, I discovered that *I'm the motor*.)

Why do I explain all this? To point out that many of us spend more time reading up on, researching, and seeking wisdom about decisions that are of low-to-moderate importance—like what bike to purchase, which car or SUV to drive, what clothes to wear for a special occasion, what shrubs or flowers to plant in the garden, which university to attend, or (you fill in the blank)—than we do on monumental issues like where our faith is currently focused, and whether it's well placed or ought to be redirected to more deserving objects and tenets of trust.

Don't you think it is worth spending some significant time reflecting on your faith?

Let me join you. My goal is to help you think through what kind of beliefs are worth choosing and to understand which criteria are helpful, or not helpful, in making that decision. In other words, I'm not so much trying to show you what to believe—everybody is constantly doing that—as I am trying to coach you in how to figure it out, weighing the various methods of choosing, and only then looking at some of the actual information to consider.

Don't you think it is worth spending some significant time reflecting on your faith?

This is crucial, because the approach you use to make your selection has a huge bearing on the outcome of your decision. You owe it to yourself not only to think about what your final choice will be, but to first step back and *think about how you're thinking about it*.

Most people never consider this. They just arbitrarily pick

up an approach (or accept one that's been handed to them) and uncritically employ it to select a belief system that may or may not be the best one. I'm sure you don't want to follow their pattern. That's why we're going to examine six different approaches, or what we're describing as six "faith paths," that people characteristically take in order to arrive at their spiritual point of view.

Once you've identified which faith path you're on, you'll be ready to evaluate whether that path is serving you well, or whether you should consider other, more reliable routes toward discovering what's true and worth trusting.[6]

I don't know where this important journey will take you—but it's imperative that you invest real time and energy in this vital area of your life in order to make certain you choose your faith wisely. I'm confident that you'll be really glad you did.

CHAPTER TWO

"THIS IS *MY* TRUTH— YOU FIND YOUR OWN"

Pragmatism, Relativism, and the Way Things Are

Atheist Richard Dawkins: "The onus is on you to say why you believe in something. There's an infinite number of gods you could believe in. I take it you don't believe in Zeus or Apollo or Thor, you believe in presumably the Christian God—"

Commentator Bill O'Reilly: "Jesus! Jesus was a real guy, I can see him—"

Dawkins: "Yeah—"

O'Reilly: "I know what he did. And so I'm not positive that Jesus is God, but I'm throwing in with Jesus, rather than throwing in with you guys, because you guys can't tell me how it all got here. You guys don't know."

Dawkins: "We're working on it. Physicists are—"

O'Reilly: "When you get it, then maybe I'll listen."

Dawkins: "Well now, if you look at the history of science over the centuries, the amount that's gained in knowledge each century is stupendous. In the beginning of the twenty-first century, we don't know everything, we have to be humble. We have to, in humility, say that there's a lot that we still don't know—"

O'Reilly: "All right, when you guys figure it out, then you come back here and tell me, because until that time I'm sticking with Judeo-Christian philosophy and my religion of Roman Catholicism, because it helps me as a person—"

Dawkins: "Ah, that's different. If it helps you, that's great. That doesn't mean it's true."

O'Reilly: "Well, it's true for me. You see, I believe—"

Dawkins: "You mean true for you is different from true for anybody else?"

O'Reilly: "Yeah, absolutely—"

Dawkins: "Something's either got to be true or not!"

O'Reilly: "No, no. I can't prove to you that Jesus is God, so that truth is mine and mine alone, but you can't prove to me that Jesus is not, so you have to stay in your little belief system. . . ."[1]

It was a brief but fascinating exchange on *The O'Reilly Factor* television program between two colorful and outspoken individuals. It also seemed like a classic example of two ships passing in the night. These men were talking to each other in plain English, and they were using the same word—*truth*—but they clearly weren't using the same dictionary to define what they meant by the term.

This question about the nature of truth goes back at least as far as the Greek philosophers Plato and Aristotle. And it came up again during the trial of Jesus, when Pilate, the Roman leader, asked Jesus a seemingly simple question: "What is truth?"[2] We can only wish that Pilate would have waited for a clear answer to his question before walking out of his palace room, because here we are, two thousand years later, still scratching our heads over the very same issue.

Let's think about this. If you look at what Bill O'Reilly was saying, he was claiming that for him, at least in this situation, truth is *what works*. This is what we would call a *pragmatic* approach. He said, "I'm sticking with Judeo-Christian philosophy and my religion of Roman Catholicism, because it helps me as a person . . . it's true for me. . . . I can't prove to you that Jesus is God, so that truth is mine and mine alone. . . ." This set of beliefs is satisfying and seems to be working for O'Reilly, so he declares that it's his own truth.

People talk that way all the time: Whatever you believe "is *true for you.*" It's as if we can each have our own private reality. And it's an equal-opportunity way of thinking, because, as they often tell you, "You have your truth, and I have mine." As long as you're each sincere in your beliefs, the theory goes, and your beliefs are "working for you," then whatever you believe is true for you, even if your so-called truths are contradictory to mine or someone else's. As one Hollywood screenwriter summed it up, "Whatever the truth is in you . . . you have to be true to *that* truth."[3]

This pragmatic, relativistic approach to faith is so popular these days that we're highlighting it as the first of the six paths we'll be discussing in this book. For simplicity, we'll refer to it as the *Relativistic* faith path. As we'll see, it's a hard one to actually live out—but that doesn't keep people from choosing their faith based on what seems to work best for them and fits their own way of seeing things.

Sophisticated thinkers will sometimes describe the Relativistic path in terms of differing truths that are based on personal perception and experience. They explain that truth is *perspectival*. For example, the way you see the world and the way a poor peasant woman in Peru sees the world are going to be completely different. Her truth will be very different from your truth. All of us are limited to our own ideas. Nobody else can see things through your eyes, and you can't see the world through anyone else's eyes. No one can access the world in a way that gives an objective view, seeing the big picture outside of the limits of our own personal perspectives. So "truth" is what fits each person's own particular perspective and set of beliefs. In effect, these people are emphasizing that truth is not so much what *works* for you, but *what fits* for you. As long as something coheres with the rest of your personal understanding of things—your worldview—then it's true for you but not necessarily for anyone else.

I should point out that this theory speaks as if it can actually see the bigger picture of how we all think, and thus presents itself as the exception that rises above its own rule. In other words, if someone says that all truth is limited to one's own point of view, then the claim itself—that all truth is perspectival—must itself be limited to the speaker's point of view, and thus is not relevant to or binding on the rest of us.

But if it *is* relevant to and binding on the rest of us, then it is the exception that proves that all truth is *not* perspectival. This is a serious, self-defeating contradiction within the Relativistic approach.

It's also interesting to note that the proponents of the Relativistic view attempt to persuade the rest of us to adopt *their* view—trying, in effect, to move us from our own perspectival positions regarding truth over to theirs. This alone unveils a major inconsistency in their theory, revealing the fact that the promoters of this view really do believe that at least some ideas and realities are objective enough to allow us to rise above our individual perspectives to see more-or-less the same thing and have a meeting of the minds. So, if that's supposed to be the case with their sophisticated theory of truth, why could it not also be the case with many other, simpler things that we all experience and believe? I think it *is* the case, so we are therefore justified in dispensing with the Relativistic theory altogether.

The Relatvistic approach tries to carve up the truth pie in a way that allows everyone to enjoy their own slice of it.

But setting aside for the moment the issue of self-contradiction within the Relativistic faith path, I will admit that this way of thinking does have some appeal. It seems to have the potential for stopping a lot of bickering between people who want to argue about whose perspective is right or wrong. Instead, the Relativistic approach tries to carve up the truth pie in a way that allows everyone to enjoy their own slice of it—and thus, at least theoretically, allowing everybody to get along. It's like the old saying, "You go your way and I'll go mine, and if our paths should ever meet again, it would be beautiful." Certainly, in our world of increasingly radical religious and political fundamentalism, we could use a lot more of just getting along, as we each do our own thing while mutually accepting and supporting other people as they do their own thing.

That all seems pretty positive at first blush. But if I'm really honest about it, I don't fully comprehend what it actually means. Seriously—I just can't get my mental arms around it. (Sorry about the mixed metaphor, but you know what I mean . . . about not knowing what I mean . . . right?)

So I decided to consult some experts. I looked up *relativism* in my copy of the 541-page *Blackwell Companion to Philosophy* (I just *knew* I'd find a practical use for that weighty tome eventually). Here's a portion of what it said:

> Concerning the notion of *relative truth* . . . it is very difficult to make sense of it. An assertion that a proposition is "true for me" (or "true for members of my culture") is more readily understood as a claim about what I (or members of my culture) *believe* than it is as a claim ascribing to that proposition some peculiar form of truth.[3]

So, you see, even these really smart experts in philosophy admit that relativistic ideas are hard to make sense of. So, at least I'm not alone.

Now, I do understand and support one aspect of it—the "getting along" part. I'm all for tolerance of other people's beliefs. I'll fight for the civil rights of the wide spectrum of religions and spiritual practices—including ones that might seem strange and even a bit wacky to me—as long as they're not hurting people.

As the title of this book suggests, I genuinely believe in letting each person choose his or her own faith, with the hope that in the marketplace of ideas, the more worthwhile ones will rise to the top. It's part of what I love about Western culture— the freedom to think about and weigh ideas and to decide for ourselves. But supporting the legal right of a wide gamut of religions and *-isms* to exist and operate freely is not the same as thinking they're all *true*. It's simply acknowledging that we see things differently, while still agreeing to like each other. And talk to each other. And listen to each other's points of view. And maybe even learn some things from each other along the way.

Religious tolerance is a very good thing; but saying that *everybody's beliefs are true* is, in my mind, incomprehensible.

Let me illustrate why that is. If I try to apply the relativistic philosophies of "*what works* for me is true" or "*what fits* for me is true" directly to the O'Reilly/Dawkins dialogue, I would have to conclude that, for Dawkins, God really does not exist, because Dawkins doesn't

I genuinely believe in letting each person choose his or her own faith, with the hope that in the marketplace of ideas, the more worthwhile ones will rise to the top.

believe in him (or her, or it). But at the same time, and in an equally real way, the Christian God *does* exist for Bill O'Reilly, because O'Reilly really, sincerely believes in that God.

Do you see the problem? Under this scenario, God does and does not exist at the same time, for two different people, based on their own particular beliefs. I know God is supposed to be able to do miracles—but pulling off simultaneous existence and nonexistence seems like a stretch, even for the Almighty.

Now, if we add to the mix a Hindu, who believes that the entire material world is illusory maya, and all is just part of the mind of the pantheistic One, then for him *everything* is God. This includes Dawkins and O'Reilly, the chairs they're sitting on, the air they're breathing, and so forth. It's all part of the all-encompassing god, whom we can't know, and who can't know us.

So, if this Hindu enters the room with Dawkins and O'Reilly, then no god/God now has to pull off a feat of simultaneity: not existing at all (the atheist perspective); existing as the personal, creator God (in Christian terms); and existing as the impersonal All (the Hindu concept). All three, all at once. And I won't even try to explain what happens when a Scientologist enters the room!

Now, I think my explanation was fair to the views of each party—including the relativists who claim to hold to this kind of a multi-truth "understanding." And as much as I'd like to be "politically correct" (or perhaps "spiritually correct") by saying that everyone in the example is right, I just can't bring myself to play that kind of a mind game.

So, let me weigh in on this question myself. Going back to the dialogue we started with, I'm afraid I have to side with Richard Dawkins, the atheist—at least this time around. Not on his final conclusions, mind you, but on his seemingly clearer and higher definition of truth, which he states so simply and clearly: "Something's either got to be true or not!"

Call me old-fashioned, but truth is just *what's real*. Not my own private reality—or yours—but the way things really are.

Truth is *what is*—what exists really exists, and what doesn't exist really doesn't exist—whether we like it or not, whether we can prove it or not, whether we have different perceptions about it, or whether we think about it or believe in it at all.

Maybe a few everyday examples will help (though you'll just have to go with me on the first one). Let's say you don't believe in trucks. You've heard about trucks, you've known people who claimed to own a truck, and you've talked to people who say they've ridden in trucks. You've even seen artists' renditions of trucks as well as alleged photographs of them. The evidence for trucks sometimes seems pretty strong—but you're still not convinced. "It's all part of a vast and clever truck-cult conspiracy," you say, "because there actually are no trucks."

Call me old-fashioned, but truth is just what's real. *Not my own private reality—or yours—but the way things really are.*

Then you decide to cross the street. You look to the left and you look to the right. No cars are coming. No motorcycles or bikes, either. Not even a horse-drawn buggy. However, there is something that looks very much like a truck barreling down the road toward you. But this doesn't fool you because, of course, you know that trucks don't exist. So you step off the curb and onto the pavement—right into the path of what you're sure is the deceptive but harmless apparition of a nonexistent truck.

So here's the question: Will your sincere "anti-truck" belief save you from the reality of the twenty-ton semi that is about to impose its very real existence on your small and oh-so-vulnerable body? Of course not! Your *what fits* disbelief is about to encounter true *what is* reality; and, like it or not, your conspiracy theories and skepticism about trucks aren't going to make a bit of difference. Reality is just that way—harsh, but so very real. Soon you'll be *wearing* that truck.

∞

I have a friend who likes to chide his relativist buddies for getting up in the morning and routinely drinking a glass of orange juice before going out and doing other things, such as filling their cars with gasoline. "If things are really relative to what you believe them to be," he says, "why don't you reverse your morning routine and drink a glass of gasoline before you fill your car with orange juice?" Seems silly, yes, but if relativism were true and the person were actually sincere in these beliefs, then it should all work out fine. I'm sure it won't surprise you to know that my friend hasn't had any takers on his suggestion so far.

Or how about this: Next time you're on a road trip that takes you down Interstate 110, decide in your mind that *what works* for you is to interpret the 110 on the sign as the speed limit. Don't do this haphazardly. Really be sincere in your belief that this is the case, knowing it works for you and fits your broader belief that automobile manufacturers install speedometers that go up to 160 miles per hour for good reason—and then step on the accelerator. It'll be a wild and exciting ride, and you'll probably get to your destination sooner.

Oh, but be ready to explain to the officer who pulls you over that *what fits* within your belief system is that the speed limit is 110 miles per hour. When he sees your sincerity and understands that this is *what works* for you, or *what fits* within your particular understanding of the world, I'm sure he'll just smile and send you on your way. Do you think? Or do you suppose he might hold you to his own truth—the *real* truth of what that "110" actually means—and hand you a ticket?

Or one more: A family member comes home late one night, looking a little disheveled and acting a bit sheepish, smelling of alcohol and in no mood to talk. When you ask what's going on, what kind of answer do you hope to get back? Would you be satisfied with a *what works* or a *what fits* response, or are you looking for a true *what is* answer?

Would you be satisfied with a what works *or a* what fits *response, or are you looking for a true* what is *answer?*

Keep in mind that the *what works* approach to truth could lead him or her to say whatever you want to hear so that you'll let up and not probe any deeper. If it gets you off the warpath, then that's *what works* at that moment. That's enough "truth" for one night. Similarly, an effective fiction writer, or even a clever and consistent liar, is able to weave together a coherent tale of *what fits* into their own system of thoughts and beliefs, but the story they tell may have nothing to do with what actually happened.

∞

Can you see why it's the old-fashioned understanding of "*true truth*" (the *what is* variety) that we really want and need to live our lives by—and that we expect others around us to live by, as well? That's the view of truth that Plato, Aristotle, Jesus, and most good thinkers have held through the ages—and it's certainly the one we apply and hold people to in our courts of law.

Our job in all of the examples above, and in any others we can think of, is to avoid inventing a fantasy reality within our own minds that we hope will then begin to magically materialize and become real. (If you think about it, that's a pretty good description of *delusion*.) Instead, *we must find out what truly is real and then align our lives and actions to that reality.*

Trucks really do exist and can run you over—so you'd be wise not to step out in front of one. Orange juice is good to drink, but gasoline can kill you—so choose your beverages carefully. The sign that says "110" on the interstate is telling you the route number, not the speed limit—and the officer in that car with the red-and-blue flashing lights will hold you accountable for understanding and abiding by the actual speed limit, relativist or otherwise. Family members who come home three sheets to the wind need to provide a truthful explanation—one that corresponds with the facts. So just fess up!

This all seems so clear and obvious, don't you think? It does, at least, until we approach the world of *spiritual matters*. Many people apply commonsense thinking to their daily lives in ordinary, concrete situations, like the examples I gave. But when it comes to values, morals, and spiritual beliefs, they revert to relativistic modes of thinking.

Why is that? Why is it that a smart guy like Bill O'Reilly can be such a hard-nosed realist about things like politics, legal issues, cultural controversies, and societal concerns, and yet revert so quickly to a pragmatic, *what works* approach to truth when he talks about his religious faith?

One reason is that religious faith enters the realm of the

invisible—of things we can't see, touch, or feel, such as God and the supernatural. These realities are harder to verify, and we can't completely prove or disprove them, so we let ourselves get mushy in our way of speaking, and even in our way of thinking. We unwittingly begin to play mind games, saying things like, "God can exist for you but not for me—and that's okay, because we're both entitled to our own truth." We talk as if religious ideas are merely some kind of utilitarian remedy or therapy designed to make us feel better but not based on anything real. I'll take an aspirin; you take a placebo—as long as our headaches go away and we both feel better, who cares?

Religious faith enters the realm of the invisible—of things we can't see, touch, or feel, such as God and the supernatural. These realities are harder to verify.

But truth isn't like that. Not in the physical realm or the spiritual realm. In both areas, *what is* is. Whatever is real in the spiritual realm was already real before you arrived. And it will remain that way, whether or not you think about it, believe it, disbelieve it, or ignore it altogether.

So if Bill O'Reilly turns out to be right about the Christian God in a real *what is* kind of way, then that same God exists for Richard Dawkins and the rest of us, even if Dawkins writes a hundred books against him. By the same token, if Richard Dawkins turns out to be right in a real *what is* kind of way about the nonexistence of a God, then the chanting of a thousand monks, the prayers of a hundred saints, the singing and dancing of scores of fired-up Pentecostals, and sincere belief from you and me—as well as the bold words of Bill O'Reilly—won't make some kind of God pop into existence.

∞

Reality is just what is. Truth, even truth about spiritual realities, is not produced by what we choose to believe in. The fact that we can't see spiritual and supernatural things doesn't make any difference concerning what's really there. What's real already exists, with or without our belief in it; we just need to discover it.

I've already alluded to this, but let me state it clearly: Sincerity doesn't change reality. I can join a mushroom cult, but my deeply trusted, sincerely felt beliefs that Jesus was a mushroom aren't going to make him a mushroom. Sincerity may be attractive, and perhaps even admirable, but let's be honest: *You can be sincere, but sincerely wrong.*

And let's be honest about something else, too. Nobody really believes it when somebody declares that "all religions are true." That's what people say when they're pretty sure nobody's going to press them on it. But the truth is, we all draw lines in the sand somewhere.

Don't believe me? Then why aren't *you* a member of the mushroom cult? It actually does exist, and they really do think that Jesus was some kind of a highly evolved mushroom. (And you thought I was making this stuff up. Welcome to the weird world of religious cults and sects!)

Or what about the Heaven's Gate UFO group? Remember those folks who moved to California (where else?), rented an upscale mansion, put on uniforms that included the now infamous black-and-white Nike running shoes, lay side by side on bunk beds, and poisoned themselves—all so they'd be freed from their bodies and ready to be picked up by a soon-to-be-arriving spaceship flying behind the comet Hale-Bopp as it moved near the earth? Sad as the outcome was, the word *wacky* isn't too strong for this one, don't you think? Speaking of poison, remember the horrific events surrounding the Jim Jones cult, in which his flock of nearly a thousand people in Guyana drank cyanide-laced Flavor Aid in order to escape scrutiny and prosecution? And what about David Koresh and his group of followers, who allowed their compound in Waco, Texas, to burn to the ground—with themselves and their families all inside?

I think we'd agree that these belief systems were wrong—even though the people in them may have been completely sincere. So we're on the same page about the fact that not all religions are true. When differing groups teach contradictory ideas about God, faith, and spiritual things, they simply can't all be right. They could all be wrong, but they can't all represent *what is*.

When differing groups teach contradictory ideas about God, faith, and spiritual things, they simply can't all be right.

Here's another reason we can't buy into the idea that everybody's "truth" is valid: Deep down, we all think *we're* right and anyone who disagrees with us is wrong. And if you disagree with that statement, you've proven my point. (If you think you're right and I'm wrong about even that, it means I was right about that in the first place.)

None of this, of course, proves who is actually right concerning their views of God, religion, and so on. It simply lays out what I think are essential ground rules: We must look for genuine truth and reality, the kind that accurately describes *what is*—even in the areas we can't see. Therefore, when we do end up choosing a faith, we want it to be one that is focused on real objects that are worthy of our trust, and not a faith based on what we hope will work for us, our own imagination, wishful thinking, or some kind of mental remedy or cop-out we've concocted to make ourselves feel better.

∞

So where should we start? First, we need to search for what's real. As the Hebrew scriptures put it, we need to "love truth."[4] Becoming a lover of truth is going to take persistence—and a certain degree of mental toughness. We have to be willing to recognize what is true, even if it flies in the face of what we've thought in the past. We have to accept the possibility that we'll end up choosing a faith that's different from what we've believed up to this point. But if we're lovers of truth, we should be willing to do so.

I like the attitude of some of the early Greek philosophers who engaged in debates over truth. Some, I'm told, would tell the audience at the outset of the debate that the best thing that could happen would be for the opposing debater to win. Why? Because, in the process, the first debater and his supporters would be helped to better see, understand, and accept truth. Discussions conducted with this mind-set were "not a contest between opponents . . . but a cooperative search for truth and understanding."[5]

So let's follow this example and let go of the convenient comfort of the Relativistic faith path. Let's stop placing our faith in *what works* and instead tenaciously track down what's really true. And once we've discovered *what is*, let's be willing to actually take the courageous step of aligning our beliefs to the truth we've discovered. As in every other area of life, in the realm of spiritual realities, we need to figure out *what is* and then adjust and conform our faith and actions to that reality.

That's the important matter we want to tackle in the following chapters: How to find the right direction in our spiritual journey—not deciding haphazardly, as people so often do, but *intentionally*, based on what's true, so we'll be able to embrace and really live with our conclusions.

CHAPTER THREE

"BUT I'VE *ALWAYS* BELIEVED WHAT I BELIEVE"

Tradition and Truth

I live in Southern California.

I know—it's regarded by the rest of the country, and perhaps by much of the world, as a land of quirky health fads and eccentric people. I don't take that personally, even if I did spend thirty-eight dollars the other day at Trader Joe's—and then realized as the cashier was bagging my purchases that I had just blown two twenties on nothing but fresh fruits and raw nuts. I guess after five years of living here, I'm pretty well acclimated to SoCal culture.

Heidi and I, along with our two teenage kids, Emma Jean and Matthew, really do love it out here. Where else can you go swimming, hiking, or mountain biking virtually every day—about fifty weeks a year? Not long ago, I was out riding my bike. I was pedaling up a long hill, doing some serious sweating, and thinking to myself how I wished it weren't so hot outside—and then I felt guilty when I realized it was *February*.

I like that we can ski in the morning on the snowy slopes of the San Bernardino Mountains, and then on the afternoon of the same day, after a short drive, we can swim along the sun-drenched shores of the Pacific Ocean. (I've never actually done this. I just enjoy knowing that I could.)

People here decorate their palm trees for the holidays. You've gotta love it—lights and tinsel hanging from the tropical foliage. Each Christmas, one of my friends turns on his air conditioner to its highest setting, waits until it gets really cold in the house, lights the fireplace, and then his whole family puts on warm sweaters and sits around shivering together, pretending that it's, like, real winter. (Please don't report this to Al Gore.)

Try not to resent us for this, but we really do live in paradise on earth.

So why is it, then, that every year when the holidays roll around, I start to feel homesick? I know that probably seems like a normal impulse to you—until you realize where the home I'm longing for actually is: *North Dakota*.

Nothing against my beloved home state or any of my family or friends who still live there, but have you ever *been* to North

Dakota? Probably not. It's the least visited tourist state in the entire Union. Seriously.

Not that it's so bad there, at least for the couple months of summer, but there really are very few actual attractions. (What about the beautiful Black Hills or majestic Mount Rushmore, you ask? Um, yeah—those are in *South* Dakota.)

The people there seem to be aware of this problem. In fact, there was a serious move a few years back to change the name of the state by dropping the *North* and just calling it "Dakota." Nobody seemed to realize that they were trying to change the wrong word. *North* Carolina, for example, doesn't have this kind of a perception problem. My suggestion, in case anyone is interested, is to deal with the truly troublesome part—which is *Dakota*—and just change the name to "North Florida." That should help.

Another problem is that the state is simply not on the way to anywhere. Unless you need to drive the hundreds of miles from Minnesota to Montana, or perhaps take a trek from Sioux Falls to Saskatoon, you're not likely to cross NoDak country. I mean, you've got to be intentional about it. Not to mention that there's basically only one airline that flies there, and for the price of the ticket you could probably fly to Paris or Prague.

Did I mention the winters? My brother-in-law, Glen, who lives twenty-three miles from the Canadian border, describes it like this: "We have nine months of winter, and then we have three months of really bad snowmobiling." The week my wife and I got married in Velva, which is sort of a suburb of my hometown of Minot, the wind chill got all the way down to ninety degrees below zero. We *had* to get married—just to stay warm and survive.

I discovered the ultimate symbol of a North Dakota winter one day when my father-in-law, Hillis, was visiting our home in California and I noticed some scratches on the tops of his leather walking shoes. "Hillis," I asked, "what happened to your new shoes?" In all seriousness he said, "Oh, those are from the chains I have to clamp on when I'm at home, so I can go for walks through the snow and ice."

I think you're getting my point: North Dakota is a cold, out-of-the-way place. One that not a lot of people even *try* to get to—especially people who live in warm places like California. And yet I still get strangely homesick for it around the holidays. It has gotten so bad lately that I've come really close to throwing the entire family into the car—spur-of-the-moment—along with all the Christmas gifts, parkas, sweaters, scarves and gloves, boots, tire chains, and even the dog, so we could risk our lives and drive almost two thousand miles through the desert, over the mountains, and onto the ice-packed highways straight into the tundra in order to get up to Heidi's and my parents' houses for the holidays.

Thankfully, I've come to my senses just in the nick of time, put another string of lights on the palm tree, poured myself a glass of eggnog, and phoned our snowbound relatives instead. But one thing's for sure: *Tradition* is a powerful magnet. Especially when that tradition involves the place we call home.

∞

One of the most haunting pieces of literature I've ever read was a short story called "The Lottery," written by Shirley Jackson in the late 1940s. The basic story line is this: In a small, old-fashioned, and seemingly friendly town of about three hundred people, they have an annual practice that goes back further than anyone can remember. The residents gather together at the same time each year, and the head of each household draws a piece of paper out of a splintered, old, black wooden box. Because it's a small, close-knit community, they know exactly how many families will be part of the lottery. They put just the right number of pieces of paper in the box—all blank, except one, which has a black spot on it.

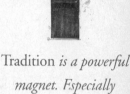

The unfortunate family that draws the piece of paper with the spot on it then has to bring every member of their household, from youngest to oldest—small children included—back up to the box to draw pieces of paper, again with just one piece having the spot on it. This time, whichever unlucky soul happens to get the marked piece of paper is immediately turned upon by the entire crowd—every man, woman, and child, including the victim's own family—and is summarily stoned to death.

Tradition is a powerful magnet. Especially when that tradition involves the place we call home.

In the story, Tessie Hutchinson, a beloved and respected community member, wife of Bill Hutchinson, and mother of three, draws the ill-fated ballot. The tale ends as she screams, "It isn't fair! It isn't right!"

And then we're told that the townspeople "were upon her."

What's interesting is that none of the characters even questions why they do this horrible thing each year. In fact, when a man named Mr. Adams mentions to a senior townsman called Old Man Warner that "over in the north village they're thinking of giving up the lottery," the old man's response is stern and strong and gives a hint of the superstition that backs up the town's terrible tradition.

"Pack of crazy fools," he replies. "Listening to the young folks, nothing's good enough for them. Next thing you know, they'll be wanting to go back to living in caves, nobody work any more, live that way for a while. Used to be a saying about 'Lottery in June, corn be heavy soon.' First thing you know, we'd all be eating stewed chickweed and acorns. *There's always been a lottery.*"[1]

∞

As frightening as that fictional story is, it illustrates the sobering truth about traditions. They're just habits, sometimes older than memory, and they're often accepted without question or even real thought. "Why challenge it?" the reasoning goes. "It's the way we've always done things around here."

Traditions are just habits, sometimes older than memory, and they're often accepted without question or even real thought. "It's the way we've always done things around here."

Traditions can be very positive, like an old family custom, familiar patterns, and surroundings that make you feel at home—or practices like giving supplies to people who are in need around the holidays or offering hospitality to people who lack food or shelter.

Traditions can also be neutral—neither helpful nor harmful—like the story of the woman who cooked a Sunday roast for her family. Before putting the roast in the pan she would always cut off the ends of the meat. One time, as she was doing this, her daughter asked, "Mom, why do you cut off the ends of the roast before you put it in the pan?" Her answer was, "Well, that's just what you have to do." But the girl persisted. "Why? Does it make it taste better or cook more evenly?" she asked. "I really don't know; it's just what Grandma always did. I do it that way because it's what she taught me. When we visit her, let's ask her why."

So the next time they were with Grandma, they asked her why she always trimmed the ends off of roasts before putting them in the oven. Puzzled, she said, "I don't do that." With a surprised look the mother insisted, "Yes, you do, and that's what you taught me to do years ago when you showed me how to prepare a roast."

"Oh," the grandmother replied with a chuckle, "I used to have to do that because back then I had such a small pan—it was the only way I could make a large roast fit."

Funny story, but funnier still how many things we do in our own lives that are like that. "Well, that's just what you have to do," we reassure ourselves.

Traditions can also be negative and yet be passed down just as blindly as any other. Certainly that was true in "The Lottery," but it's often that way in real life as well.

Many of our grandparents, for example, used to make demeaning remarks about people of different skin color; or they'd lump together certain ethnic groups under one negative banner. They weren't necessarily trying to be mean-spirited, but they were passing on the stereotypes they had picked up from their own relatives and friends. "Oh, it's best that those folks stick together with their own kind, on their own side of town," they'd say. "Some of them can be nice enough as people, but you wouldn't want them living in your neighborhood or attending your house of worship." And, they might add, "Just watch out if you ever have to do business with one of them. You've got to watch 'em like a hawk."

These ugly prejudices get passed on, generation to generation. About the time we think we're finally free of them, an old label or expression will come up somewhere in a conversation, and we realize this is one tradition we must continually and tenaciously root out.

∞

Another "tradition" that some of us had handed down from our relatives was the habit of smoking several packs of cigarettes a day. Years ago, this was considered fashionable, a way to fit in, and the cigarettes didn't cost much back then, either. Why not just light up like everyone else? Then, as more and more people got sick, and evidence began to mount that these "cancer sticks" really can kill you, smoking proved to be a very hard habit to break. Many of us lost our grandparents prematurely as a result. Unfortunately, many of our parents "inherited" their harmful nicotine habits, and even after the avalanche of incriminating evidence came out about the devastating impact of using tobacco, many from my generation—and the next—still find themselves addicted to cigarettes today.

The same kind of generational hand-me-down habits are seen in a variety of other damaging arcas:

- alcohol and drug addictions

- negative attitudes toward people of different religions or gender

- poor and sometimes destructive communication patterns

- tendencies toward overworking and underresting

- parental neglect of children

- unhealthy eating and exercise routines (or lack of exercise)

- psychological or physical abusiveness between family members

What's challenging is to find the balance between giving the respect and honor that is due our elders while not emulating their bad behaviors. It's important to love them, but also to step back and make an honest assessment of what they are doing, or have done, especially before we uncritically lock into their patterns of thinking and living. We need to candidly ask ourselves, "How did their beliefs and actions really work out for them? Do I want to see similar results in my own life?"

If we're to resist passing down through the generations what my friend Bill Hybels calls "a broken baton" of harmful habits, beliefs, and attitudes, then we'll have to back up and consider our own lives very carefully—and probably make some challenging course corrections along the way.

∞

Nowhere in our lives is a careful, critical evaluation more needed than in the area of *faith*. Most of us grew up with some kind of inherited spirituality, whether Christian, Muslim, Hindu, Buddhist, or even a nonspiritual faith like atheism. I think this *Traditional* faith path is the most common approach people employ to "choose" their faith—though it's really not a choice at all because it's just passively received. It's usually adopted as a hand-me-down religion that has never been critically examined.

One way or another, you were initiated, baptized, consigned, or commissioned into a particular set of religious beliefs or practices (even if it's the beliefs and practices of atheism, which some practice quite religiously). Today you might wear the label of whatever group those practices represent, but, if pressed, you

couldn't give an authentic reason why you think you're in the right faith. For you, it's just a tradition—which might be why you often feel halfhearted and noncommittal about your beliefs. It's hardly accurate to call them your own.

The Traditional *faith path is the most common approach people employ to "choose" their faith— though it's really not a choice at all because it's just passively received.*

Now, that doesn't necessarily make the faith you grew up with wrong or bad. But if you got it as a hand-me-down, then it's sort of the luck of the draw. If you think about it, you're just banking on the hope that somewhere back in your family history, some-

body—your mother or father, a grandparent, or an earlier an-cestor—carefully examined the whole realm of questions about God, spirituality, and *what is* before coming to a conclusion about faith.

But that's a huge roll of the dice. Because, well, let's be honest: These are the same people who were also working sixty or eighty hours a week in order to get by, moving from place to place trying to find a better life, learning new cultures and maybe even a new language, and perhaps (going back to our earlier list) trying to overcome their inbred prejudices, strug-gling with various addictions, fighting with other family mem-bers or factions of society, and so forth. How much time and effort do you think they really gave to serious reflection about spiritual realities? The answer is that they probably didn't give this vitally important area nearly the focus it deserves—and maybe not even as much, going back to chapter 1, as I gave to researching and buying my new carbon-fiber-framed mountain bike. And yet, far too readily, we're prone to accept what they handed down to us as being absolute, gospel truth.

Juxtapose that reality with the famous words of Socrates when he warned us that "the unexamined life is not worth living."

We must beware of turning our traditions—or our family background, heritage, or ethnicity—into an excuse to blindly perpetuate something that may or may not be healthy, helpful, or even true. The philosophy of "that's just what you have to do" simply doesn't cut it when it comes to choosing your faith.

A philosopher named Paul Copan, who is an expert in these matters, was asked whether we aren't culturally conditioned to just accept and live with the beliefs we grew up with, regardless of what they are. The question was posed to him like this: "Isn't it true that if you were born in Saudi Arabia, you'd probably be a Muslim, or if you were born in India, you'd probably be a Hindu?"

"Statistically speaking, that could be true," Copan replied. "And if the pluralist had grown up in medieval France or modern Somalia, he probably wouldn't be a pluralist. So the geography argument doesn't carry much weight. Besides, I could make the claim that if you lived in Nazi Germany, the chances are you would have been part of the Hitler Youth. Or if you lived in Stalin's Russia, you would have been a Communist. But does that mean Nazism or Communism is as good a political system as democracy? No—just because there has been a diversity of political systems through history doesn't prevent us from concluding that one political system is superior to its rivals. Presumably, there are good reasons for preferring one political system over another. There are good reasons for rejecting a system like Nazism or Communism in favor of democracies. So why can't it be the same with regard to religious beliefs? The point is: Are there good reasons for believing one religious viewpoint over another?"[2]

∞

If there's a real God who has given us the necessary clues and information, and who expects us to figure out who he is and genuinely follow him, then it's not going to work to face him someday and say, "As you're aware, I was raised Irish Catholic, so I was never really allowed to contemplate any other options." Or, "I come from a long line of devout Buddhists, so it was simply unthinkable in my family that any of us would ever become anything other than a Buddhist." Or, "We're Jewish, you know, so we could never really read or consider the teachings of Jesus—it just wouldn't have been kosher." Or, "Well, you know, I grew up a Calvinist, so I never really had the freedom or ability to choose otherwise."

"There are good reasons for preferring one political system over another. Are there good reasons for believing one religious viewpoint over another?"

But what if the Catholics are right, or the Buddhists, or even the backwoods snake handlers? How would you know unless you stepped back and actually tested the teachings of the various faith traditions?

It's interesting that Jesus, who at minimum was one of the

greatest religious leaders of all time, was also one of the hardest on tradition. Listen to his surprisingly stinging words, aimed at the spiritual authorities of his day and recorded in one of four early biographies:

> So the Pharisees and teachers of religious law asked him, "Why don't your disciples follow our age-old tradition? They eat without first performing the hand-washing ceremony."
>
> Jesus replied, "You hypocrites! Isaiah was right when he prophesied about you, for he wrote, 'These people honor me with their lips, but their hearts are far from me. Their worship is a farce, for they teach man-made ideas as commands from God.' For you ignore God's law and substitute your own tradition."[3]

If you read this story in its surrounding context, you'll see that Jesus was so incensed with the Pharisees and teachers of the law that he repeated his indictment against blindly following tradition three times in one short conversation. Apparently, he saw the spiritual devastation that resulted from blindly following the beliefs and edicts of earlier generations, and he wanted to jolt his listeners into a more careful consideration of these matters. For him, it was much more important to get it right than to keep the peace, gloss over problems, or fit into familial or cultural expectations. And, interestingly, he was echoing prior warnings given centuries earlier through the prophet Isaiah, who wrote, "The Lord says, 'These people say they are mine. They honor me with their lips, but their hearts are far from me. And their worship of me is nothing but man-made rules learned by rote.'"[4]

So the question for us is this: Are we willing to step back

and examine our inherited beliefs and make sure that we've thoughtfully and intentionally chosen a faith worth following?

Here's the point we need to grapple with: *Our parents could have been wrong!* And their parents could have been wrong before them. My parents could have been wrong, and the same goes for yours. And our religious leaders and teachers might also have been wrong.

I know that's hard to swallow, but stay with me here.

Looking at things more broadly, *somebody's* parents and teachers *have to be* wrong. Why? Because so many contradict each other. As we know, and as we'll discuss further in an upcoming chapter on logic, "opposites cannot both be true." This "law of noncontradiction" is an inescapable reality—and you can't even argue about it without implicitly agreeing with me. (I say this because you can't dispute the laws of logic without employing the very same laws. In fact, you can't even *think* about disputing the laws of logic without using them—so just give it up.)

Here's the point we need to grapple with: Our parents could have been wrong! *And our religious leaders and teachers might also have been wrong.*

In applying this principle of noncontradiction to matters of faith, the personal God of Judaism and Christianity is not compatible with the impersonal Brahman of Hinduism. Either God is an intelligent deity, who is distinct from the universe that he made, or he is an unconscious and impersonal pantheistic god, who is in and part of everything—*or neither* description is true—but he can't be *both* in any meaningful sense. Both concepts could be wrong, of course, but they can't both be right because they are incompatible and contradictory.

Again, we should enthusiastically support the legal right of both of these traditions (and others) to exist and to spread their messages. That's *tolerance*, which is great. But don't confuse tolerance with *truth*. There can't be two contradictory-but-true realities in the sense of genuine, *what is* truth. I feel so politically incorrect and out-of-fashion saying this, but reality is reality—it's *what is*—and we had better just come to grips with it.

To be fair, I had to face this same reality myself—as I mentioned—when I was in college. "Truths" that I had been raised to believe, and that I had always considered to be rock solid, were being challenged by a professor who seemed to know more about the subject than most of the spiritual teachers and influencers in my life. I sensed that I was no match for this man, and the people I talked to about it at my church weren't much help either. So what was I to do?

∞

When faced with the possibility that something you've been taught all your life might actually be wrong, it's tempting to try various defense maneuvers as a means of justifying and clinging to your traditions. Avoidance is one of those tactics—doing all you can to get away from the person or influence that is causing you to question. Maybe if you don't think about it, or don't get near that person or place—maybe if you just put a pillow over your head—the challenge will disappear. But then the problem is left to fester beneath the surface, causing doubt and insecurity to spread like a cancer.

Other people respond by getting indignant or angry: "Who

are you to say that *your* way is right and mine is wrong? How arrogant of you!" Such a reaction might feel good at first—at least for a few minutes. But in the end, the questions still linger. And deep down you know that it really is possible that the other person's beliefs could be right—and that you have been taught things that are wrong (even though they were sincerely believed by your parents or others who influenced you).

Wouldn't it be freeing to relax and just admit that being wrong is a possibility? Isn't it better to lower your defenses for a minute and decide that you would rather be a lover of truth than merely a defender of a tradition? Wouldn't you rather know that you are sincerely seeking an accurate picture of spiritual things and building your beliefs on ideas that are supported by the evidence?

∞

It's not necessary to become a spiritual iconoclast, challenging every authority or discarding every tradition, just because they seem old-fashioned. Rather, you can, and should, maintain respect for your family and friends who may see things differently from how you are beginning to see them. Recognize that most of us start out with beliefs that were simply handed down to us, and it's a natural part of growing up and thinking like an adult to step back and evaluate the validity of the faith you've inherited. You must decide to weigh the reasons and evidence for what you have so readily accepted up to now—so you can be sure that you end up with a faith that really makes sense because it's based on actual truth.

That was the course of action I chose to take in college. To the best of my ability, I lowered my defenses, opened my mind, and began a process of examining the very foundations of the beliefs I had been taught. And frankly, that was an uncomfortable season. The only thing that seemed worse than the idea of abandoning the beliefs I'd been raised with was the thought of basing my faith on teachings I genuinely doubted were true.

So for a time I lived within this mental purgatory, while I vigorously went to work reading books, listening to audio recordings, researching answers, and interacting with wise and studied people who could contribute to my understanding. I thoroughly tested my traditions with logic, evidence, and frequent prayers for guidance along the way, trusting that the truth would somehow end up rising to the top.

Wouldn't you rather know that you are sincerely seeking an accurate picture of spiritual things and building your beliefs on ideas that are supported by the evidence?

This process led eventually to a reaffirmation of my childhood beliefs as well as to a deepening and maturing of my faith. But that result was not guaranteed at the outset. In hindsight, the doubts and challenges I wrestled with proved to be like infections that helped to produce "spiritual antibodies" in me as I studied, reflected on, and responded to them. In the end, I was stronger for having undergone this time of searching, probing, and testing and was more confident in the faith I'd embraced.

For my close friend Lee, the opposite happened. He had come to accept a worldview that was secular, skeptical, and had no room for a big-*G* God, little-*g* gods, or any form of higher intelligence. He was a spiritual doubter who, over time, actually began to reexamine—and eventually to doubt—his own doubts. The catalyst for this change was the example set by his wife, who, after coming to faith in God, gently challenged Lee to take another look at what he believed.

I was stronger for having undergone this time of searching, probing, and testing and was more confident in the faith I'd embraced.

His natural reaction to this process was to get angry. He often slammed doors, belittled his wife's newfound faith, lashed out against her church, and gradually increased his use and abuse of alcohol. One day, in his frustration, he even kicked a hole in their living room wall.

Gradually, however, Lee settled down and let his reason begin to respond, instead of simply reacting according to his emotions. To this day, he'll tell you that it was not fun having his atheistic traditions challenged. And he didn't like the thought of acknowledging a God who, once allowed through the door, would want to have a say in how he lived his life each and every day.

But, somehow, Lee found the humility—and the persistence—to wrestle with his spiritual questions, to examine the variety of purported answers, and to carefully weigh the evidence, both pro and con. It took him nearly two years. In the end, instead of reaffirming his particular form of atheistic "faith," he had a complete change of mind. Or, as he puts it today, he experienced "a rush of reason." His wife, Leslie, describes it more as a miraculous change of heart. Today, Lee is a devout person of faith, and he writes books and speaks to groups all over the world, helping others who are on spiritual journeys similar to his own.[5]

I don't know what your outcome will be. It could be a reaffirmation of the teachings and traditions you grew up with, as it was for me. Or it could be a redirection of your thinking toward fresh beliefs and understandings, as it was for Lee. But I'll tell you one thing for certain: Both Lee and I are glad we embarked on the adventure of spiritual discovery. We're thankful we did what it took to examine our beliefs and our backgrounds and to carefully and deliberately choose our own faith. I'm confident you will be thankful, as well.

∞

On a different day and in a different setting from the situation in which Jesus chided his listeners for their blind allegiance to tradition, he gave us each a challenge:

> Keep on asking, and you will receive what you ask for. Keep on
> seeking, and you will find. Keep on knocking, and the door will
> be opened to you. For everyone who asks, receives. Everyone
> who seeks, finds. And to everyone who knocks, the door will
> be opened.[6]

That challenge comes with an encouraging promise, and as we'll see later, Jesus has some impressive credentials that make him a trustworthy source of guidance on these important matters. In the chapters to follow, we'll also look at some tools that will help us appropriately test the teachings we grew up with.

If you're finding yourself resistant to the idea of testing your beliefs, consider the following questions:

Aren't you glad that Galileo didn't just accept the traditional understanding about the earth and the solar system and instead tested that tradition and came to a better understanding? And isn't is a good thing that some courageous explorers centuries ago bucked conventional wisdom about the earth being flat and

instead went out boldly and discovered new lands? And aren't you thankful that Thomas Edison relinquished the tradition of cursing the darkness and experimented some ten thousand times until he managed to come up with a better way to light a room?

Aren't you glad that Galileo didn't just accept the traditional understanding about the earth and the solar system and instead tested that tradition and came to a better understanding?

I'm glad about these things, too, but I don't think any of them is ultimately as important as testing our own spiritual traditions, searching for real truth, and finally choosing our faith based on proven information and open-eyed wisdom.

Before we get stuck hanging on to what is old, we might be wise to listen to the one who said, "Look, I am making everything new!"[7]

CHAPTER FOUR

"YOU'D *BETTER* BELIEVE IT!"

Authority and Reality

It was a first for me. I had never been inside a mosque before, and neither had most of the people who were taking the tour with me. We were cordially welcomed, shown around the premises, and then ushered into a large room and asked to sit down on the floor.

Soon the imam, dressed in white, stepped to the front of the room and began to speak to us. He passionately communicated with a strong, confident voice. He explained some of the tenets of Islam, and then he described how Muslims pray, worship in the mosque, and live out their faith in daily life.

Then his gaze grew intense—even stern—as he addressed some issues pertinent to Christians. "It is important for you to know that Allah is the one and only God, and that Muhammad, peace be upon him, was his true prophet. God is not divided, and he does not have a son," he declared emphatically. "Jesus, peace be upon him, was *not* the Son of God. He was a true prophet, like Muhammad, and we are to honor him—but we must never worship him. We worship Allah and Allah alone."

He went on speaking to our group a bit longer, wrapped up his comments, and then said he'd be willing to take some questions. People asked about a variety of topics, some surface level and others more substantive. The imam patiently responded to each one. As I listened, I wrestled silently with an issue that I was sure would go to the heart of what he had said and to the core of the difference between his faith and my own.

I knew that Islamic teachings say that Jesus not only was not the Son of God, but also never even made such a claim. Further, they declare that Jesus did not die on the cross, because, as I've heard Muslims explain it, "God would never allow one of his prophets to face such shame and disgrace." Also, because they don't believe in the crucifixion of Jesus, they obviously don't believe in the resurrection claims about him, either. I decided that these issues were too important to let this opportunity go by, so I raised my hand to ask my question.

"I'm curious about something," I said. "Jesus' followers walked and talked with him for several years. They also reported that he repeatedly claimed to be the Son of God, that they watched him die on the cross, and that three days later they saw and talked and ate with him after he was resurrected. We have detailed accounts of what they heard and saw. These have been preserved in literally thousands of manuscript documents that attest to these realities.

"So, we have all of this written testimony from the people who were companions of Jesus, each affirming that he claimed to be the Son of God, died on a cross, and rose from the dead. Now, correct me if I'm wrong, but what Islam teaches us about Jesus seems to be based on the words of one man, Muhammad, who, six hundred years after the time of Christ, was sitting in a cave when, as he claimed, an angel spoke to him and told him these things weren't so.

Very few people land on their particular spiritual point of view through careful consideration of the logic and evidence supporting it.

"What I'm curious about is whether you have any historical or logical reasons why we should accept that viewpoint over and against the actual historical record?"

The imam looked at me intently. After a pause, he declared resolutely, *"I choose to believe the prophet!"*—and the discussion was over. This sounded to me a lot like, "I've got my mind made up, so don't try to confuse me with the facts." For him, the influences of his religion and its founder were all he needed. He seemed like an intelligent and articulate person, but if he had deeper reasons backing up his commitment to his faith, he had chosen not to share them.

∞

The truth is that very few people land on their particular spiritual point of view through careful consideration of the logic and evidence supporting it. Most accept it either because they grew up with it (as we discussed in the previous chapter about the Traditional faith path) or because influential people in their lives expect and even demand it of them—whether they be devout Muslims; Jehovah's Witnesses who go door-to-door tirelessly talking about God's theocratic kingdom; North Koreans who worship and revere their deceased "great leader," Kim Il Sung; or compliant Christians who feel compelled by powerful teachers or influencers to "stay true to the Lord," whether that makes sense to them or not.

This approach to choosing your beliefs is what I'll call the *Authoritarian* faith path. It is similar to the Traditional faith path in that it's hard to call it a "choice," because it's usually just passively received. But the difference between the two is that the Traditional approach is more about a *habit* that gets passed on from one generation to the next, whereas the Authoritarian approach is based on *submission* to a religious leader—past or present—and the ideas that leader holds up as the standard to live by.

It's natural that you may have grown up under some sort of spiritual or religious authority, and when you were younger you just accepted what you were taught without really critically analyzing it. But part of reaching maturity in these matters is to come to the point where you step back and take a more careful look. You say to yourself, "This might have seemed right in my life up until now—but I need to really examine who and what it is that I'm following to see if it really warrants my ongoing trust and loyalty."

It's interesting that the original meaning of the Arabic word *Islam* is actually "submission," and it seems fair to say that many Muslims accept their faith primarily on the basis of the influence and authority of their parents, teachers, government, or society. Some, I'm sure, really have stepped back and tried to examine whether what they've been taught is true—and you might be one of them.

But the message that is most often communicated, at least in my observation, is an authoritative declaration that Allah is the true God, Muhammad is his messenger, and you need to submit yourself to these realities. The imam did not say to me that day, "I've carefully studied these things and have concluded, based on the evidence, that I can confidently trust the prophet." Rather, he said without further elaboration or attempt at justification, "I choose to believe the prophet," and the tone of his voice strongly implied an unspoken second half of the sentence: "and you had better just set aside your objections and choose to believe him as well."

This strong appeal to an ultimate authority can sometimes be seen in Christian circles as well. An example that stands out in my mind is the experience of Fiona, a friend of Heidi's and mine from a summer we spent in London, who later got involved in an authoritarian fundamentalist church. When I encountered her on a subsequent speaking trip to the UK, I could readily see the effects on her independence and on her normally vibrant and vivacious personality. Rather than being her usual joyful self that we'd known years earlier, Fiona had become extremely cautious. She was nervous about something as simple as coming to say hello to me at the place where I was teaching.

She did show up, but when I had the chance to sit down and talk with her, she anxiously admitted that she was fearful about being there. That was because, she told me, "I really should have gotten permission from my pastor or the church's elders to even be here, especially since I'm not sure that things I'll hear today will completely line up with what my church teaches."

I replied, with a bit of intentional naiveté, "But surely these leaders would want you to think for yourself, and learn to test ideas, and to become someone who can discern what it true and worth hanging onto—right? Isn't that part of growing up and becoming spiritually mature?"

"Surely these leaders would want you to think for yourself, and learn to test ideas, and to become someone who can discern what it true and worth hanging onto—right?"

"Actually, I don't think they would agree with that, Mark," she replied hesitantly. "I guess I wish they were more like that—though I'm not criticizing them. Mostly I think they just want all of us in the church to submit to their teaching and authority so that we'll stay away from temptations and deluding influences, and keep becoming more like Jesus. It's like the Bible talks about—being good disciples of Christ and obeying the leaders he's put over his church."

I did my best to help her see that this was an unhealthy level of control and that the Bible does not teach Christians to have that kind of blind obedience. I also tried to help her look in the mirror to see the negative impact this influence was having on her spirit and even on her physical demeanor. But she wasn't ready at that point to question or examine the teachings of these leaders or to acknowledge the ways it was hurting her as a person.

I'm glad that around that time I discovered a book called *The Subtle Power of Spiritual Abuse* and was able to send Fiona a copy.[1] I'll admit to being fearful she wouldn't read it, but rather take it to church the next Sunday and give it to her pastor. I imagined getting an irate phone call at some odd hour of the night from a fundamentalist minister with a strong English accent. But she didn't do that. I suppose because of the love and trust she felt in her friendship with Heidi and me, and the knowledge that we really cared about her, she actually did read the book. Doing so helped to gradually embolden her to do what I would encourage you to do if you've chosen your faith based on an authority in your life. Specifically, she tested the credibility of that authority and asked herself honest questions about the real impact it was having on her life. For Fiona, this led to her eventually breaking away from that controlling and spiritually stifling situation. She didn't throw away her faith, but she learned to live it out in a healthier and, I trust, more God-honoring way. Today, she's part of a great church, and she's really glad she mustered the courage to make these changes in her life.

∞

There's no doubt that blind or unquestioning reliance on authority can have negative effects on our lives—and not just in the area of faith. Think of the devastating impact that Senator Joseph McCarthy had on an entire nation when he made numerous accusations in the early 1950s against his fellow leaders in the United States government. He claimed in several speeches to be holding in his hand at that very moment a list of the names of as many as 205 employees of the State Department who were, according to him, members of the Communist Party. With the United States in the midst of the Cold War with the Soviet Union at that time, you can imagine the stir this caused. It turned into a veritable witch hunt, as endless investigations and interrogations were held, including even an inquiry into the United States Army.

McCarthy's influence became so strong that his sort of divisive tactics were given the label of *McCarthyism*—a name McCarthy himself eventually embraced. His power continued to grow to the point where political candidates soon found themselves winning or losing elections based on whether McCarthy endorsed them. Over a period of several years, many lives were disrupted, public trust was eroded, and the country endured a national nightmare—one that eventually backfired on McCarthy, as the nation's support for him and his methods quickly faded and then turned against him. In 1954, he became one of only a few U.S. senators ever to be formally censured.

And what was all of this power and authority based on? His false accusations were "supported" by a piece of paper McCarthy held up, supposedly containing a list of names of the communists who had infiltrated the government. This paper was never shown to anyone, and most of the names on it—if there were any names actually written on the paper at all—were never made public, with the very few exceptions of several people who were already known to have leftist political leanings.

Think of it: The waving of a mere piece of paper that may have been blank (or, for all we know, had McCarthy's grocery list written on it) caused years of stress, division, suspicion, and disruption in one of the most powerful governments on the planet. All based on one largely untested political authority.

What about medical authorities? I have a friend whose elderly mother, Helen, was experiencing excruciating pain in her back and shoulder. She kept getting increasingly ill until one day she started vomiting blood. They rushed her to her doctor, who gave her what seemed like a thorough examination. The diagnosis? Helen was having an allergic reaction to seasonal pollen, and she needed to take medications that would help her body deal with the allergens that were causing her so much soreness and discomfort. Relieved, the family took her back home, started her on the antihistamines and painkillers, and trusted that things would be better soon.

Well, things didn't get better; they actually got worse. Eventually, they took Helen to the emergency room to find out if something more serious might be going on. She was admitted to the hospital, and they ran her through a gamut of tests. After a couple of days, the results all came back, and they pointed to a far different diagnosis: Helen wasn't struggling with allergies; she had cancer in her lungs, bones, lymph nodes, and liver. Four days later, she was dead. Needless to say, the original doctor was one authority who needed to be tested.

How many theories have we been adamantly taught, especially in the area of science, that later were completely refuted or revised?

And what about authorities in education? How many theories have we been adamantly taught, especially in the area of science, that later were completely refuted or revised? (Or perhaps a better question might be: How many theories are we *still* being taught that are right now in the process of being discredited?) The changes in prevailing paradigms are so regular and expected that one philosopher of science, Thomas Kuhn, wrote a fascinating book about it called *The Structure of Scientific Revolutions*.[2] Unfortunately, many times the academic authorities fail to present their "truths" in light of the reality that scientific theories come and go.

And as we've illustrated in earlier chapters, both history and the daily news are filled with stories of religious authorities who overlook common sense and ignore known facts in order to teach their strange doctrines. In some cases, they even contradict the moral and ethical teachings within the allegedly holy books they claim to represent. They discredit what they say by what they do. Yet through their charismatic and sometimes powerful personalities, and perhaps some political and financial clout, they gain control over the lives of the people "under" them. Increasingly, they wield their influence to gain expanding levels of support and subservience from their flock of faithful followers. With their mix of influence and misinformation, many of these "spiritual leaders" have wreaked havoc in the daily lives of their people, not to mention the confusion they've introduced about God and matters of faith.

Harder to detect, but probably affecting many more people, are the well-meaning teachers who try to live out their faith's tenets with integrity, but who are unwittingly passing on spiritual ideas that are not well grounded in fact or history. The questionable authority in these cases is not so much the person passing it on, as it is the religious system itself, with its collection of prophets, doctrines, and holy books. These situations demand a deeper digging into the history and foundations of the faith, because there may be flaws and faulty teachings at the very root of its structure. It was this kind of issue I was raising with the imam at the mosque; I wasn't questioning his sincerity or authentic commitment to his faith. I was questioning the actual foundations of the faith's claims.

∞

At this point, you may be starting to suspect that I'm completely antiauthoritarian and would perhaps propose some sort of radical libertarianism to free us from all who would exercise influence over us. Far from it. I'm no anarchist, and I happen to think that John Cougar Mellencamp made a good point when he sang the line, "I fight authority, authority always wins."[3] The question is not *if* we'll be under authority, but to *which* authorities we'll trust and respond.

The question is not if we'll be under authority, but to which authorities we'll trust and respond.

Can you imagine a world without any authorities to lead, teach, coach, or protect us? It would be one in which you'd have to become the expert on everything, and you'd have to fend for yourself and your loved ones in every circumstance. The phrase "every man for himself" would take on a new and heightened meaning. Images of the movie *Mad Max* come to mind.

In spite of the obvious abuses of power, isn't it good we have those in government who exercise leadership in our lives—and who, more often than not, serve to protect us and to provide a civil environment in which we can do our work, raise our families, and live our lives? The Bible even says that governments are a gift from God (a challenging idea to hold onto in some situations, I realize). Aren't you thankful for medical specialists who, as a general rule, help us preserve our health? I see my doctor regularly as well as occasionally visit a chiropractor and a nutritionist. Each one has served to enrich my health, fitness, and sense of well-being. Aren't you grateful for quality educators? I've certainly spent plenty of time and money in their schools, as you have, and have benefited from most of what I've learned. The list of important authorities in our lives could be expanded almost endlessly, including law enforcement officers, honest lawyers (no, that's not an oxymoron), health inspectors, border patrolmen, marriage counselors, automobile mechanics, tax accountants, real estate appraisers, and so on.

We trust these authorities because they have the education, expertise, and experience that add up to compelling credentials. For example, we don't trust just anyone claiming to be a doctor. We trust doctors who have the right plaques up on their walls, certifying that they went to—and graduated from—the right kinds of schools, gaining training and degrees that are relevant to the needs for which we're going to them. The strength of our confidence in them is generally commensurate with the strength of their credentials.

Maybe you noticed in my earlier examples that it was actually other authorities in the same fields who brought awareness and correction to the abuses or errors. Specifically, it was other politicians who eventually censured Joseph McCarthy and reined in his influence. It was other doctors who finally diagnosed Helen's condition accurately. And it is those in the academic world of study and research who usually bring correctives to the various scientific and academic theories that we've been taught. So, when the world is working the way it seems it should, it's usually better authorities— serving as checks and balances and offering "second opinions"—who are able to improve upon the deficiencies of the previous authorities.

The same is often true in the spiritual realm. The practical challenge for us, as it relates to choosing our faith, is to muster up the courage and the clarity to reconsider and test the credentials of the spiritual authorities in our lives. These may be people or organizations that are already in leadership roles over us, or those that would like to be. We need to scrutinize what they say, teach,

The practical challenge for us is to muster up the courage and the clarity to reconsider and test the credentials of the spiritual authorities in our lives.

and do, and then compare and contrast them to other spiritual authorities, always looking to see whether they exhibit the marks of truthfulness and spiritual authenticity.

What are some of the specific criteria we can employ to put these authorities to the test? How can we apply the ancient wisdom of the apostle Paul when he warned us to "test everything that is said. Hold on to what is good. Stay away from every kind of evil"?[4]

∞

Let me offer a few key characteristics to look for in order to establish whether an authority figure, an organization—or, for that matter, the religion's founder, writings, and coleaders—has the right kind of credentials. Though this is not an exhaustive list, I trust it will provide some practical guidance out of which you can examine and then confirm or deny the authorities affecting your life of faith.

Integrity

This first characteristic might seem obvious, but it is often overlooked—especially after a person has been under someone's authority for a long time. The tendency is to let familiarity and trust grow to the point where inconsistencies or a lack of integrity are overlooked, and the leaders are treated as exceptions (and thus somehow above scrutiny) rather than as examples.

It's interesting to see what Jesus said about this in his well-known Sermon on the Mount. You don't necessarily have to view Jesus as a prophet or as the Son of God in order to recognize the wisdom in his words:

> Beware of false prophets who come disguised as harmless sheep but are really vicious wolves. You can identify them by their fruit, that is, by the way they act. Can you pick grapes from thornbushes, or figs from thistles? A good tree produces good fruit, and a bad tree produces bad fruit.[5]

We should be wary of leaders who talk a good game but who don't play by the rules themselves. If words about love, honesty, integrity, and humility (especially humility) are just that—mere words contradicted by real actions—we'd be wise to look elsewhere for guidance in matters of faith. By the same token, impeccable integrity lends credence to a leader's words and teachings.

To make this point, Jesus actually taunted his critics and accusers, challenging them to point out even one flaw or inconsistency in his life. He said, "Which of you can truthfully accuse me of sin? And since I am telling you the truth, why don't you believe me?"[6] Obviously, this isn't a challenge you want to throw out to your attackers unless you've lived an astonishingly consistent life of integrity. But his critics and accusers were left speechless. Other than making up stories and false accusations, they had nothing to say.

Now, to be fair, it's possible that a leader is simply a poor representation of the worthy faith he or she represents. But if these traits are rampant throughout the entire system, it's probably time to consider another place altogether to grow in your faith.

Consistency

This is an extension of the last point—integrity—but applied over time. *Consistency* says that integrity must be lived out over the long haul. Almost any clever person can look good for a season—like the guy on a first or second date who can dress and act in civilized ways for an evening or two. But the grind of daily life tends to reveal a person's true character.

I'm not talking about an occasional lapse that may occur and cast a shadow on a person's typically good character. I'm talking about an overall fatal flaw that proves itself over time to be impervious to challenge or correction. Leaders can and do fail, but someone with integrity and consistency will get back up, humbly acknowledge his or her mistakes, make the necessary changes, implement safeguards and accountabilities, and move forward in greater fidelity toward what is good and right. King David is an example of this. He failed miserably, but he eventually owned up to it, made important changes, and moved on. You can read his confession and sense his remorse in Psalm 51. It was his repentant attitude that led to further seasons of effective leadership in his life.

Just as it is wise in a courtship situation to look carefully and patiently at the other person to try to discern his or her real character, we should examine the life of the leader (or leaders) that represent our current or prospective faith. This includes the founder of the religion, group, or organization; national or international leaders currently at the helm; and local leaders and teachers (and the people closest to them). Try to look beneath the surface and perform frequent and honest "gut checks" to see if you might discern subtle or hidden issues. No one wants to end up following characters like Jim Jones or David Koresh, nor do we want to embrace a faith based on misguided leaders and ideas from decades or even centuries ago.

It's important to ask God for wisdom along the way. Even if you doubt that God is real or present, at least pray the skeptic's prayer.

Also, it's important to ask God for wisdom along the way. Even if you doubt that God is real or present, at least pray the skeptic's prayer. Follow the example of George Bailey in the classic movie *It's a Wonderful Life.* Here's what he prayed:

> God . . . Dear Father in Heaven, I'm not a praying man, but if you're up there and you can hear me, show me the way. I'm at the end of my rope. Show me the way, God.

Bailey is a fictional character, but just as his prayer for help was heard and answered in that powerful story, I'm confident your prayer for guidance will be answered as well.

A man once brought his son to Jesus for healing. When

Jesus told him that "anything is possible if a person believes," the father instantly uttered these transparent words to Jesus: "I do believe, but help me overcome my unbelief!"[7] It was a very vulnerable thing for the man to say, but Jesus didn't scold him for doubting. Not at all. Instead, he answered the man's sincere request and healed his son.

So, choose this semiskeptical father's words, or the prayer of George Bailey, or compose your own prayer—but it's important to actually ask God for his help and guidance as you seek wisdom on these important matters of faith.

Accuracy

Accuracy is important, because it relates to the precision and authenticity of the leader's teachings. The apostle Paul gave an *apropos* caution to his apprentice Timothy when he warned him: "Keep a close watch on how you live and on your teaching. Stay true to what is right."[8] We addressed the "how you live" part under *Integrity* and *Consistency*; now let's look at the "close watch on your teaching" part.

To put it concisely, a leader's teaching must be: (1) true to the world; (2) true to the leader's own words; and, ultimately (3) true to God's words. This last one is the most challenging, so let's start with the other two.

True to the world means that what they say about verifiable areas in the physical realm needs to prove to be accurate and true. So if a so-called holy man or holy book starts with the premise that the earth is flat, let the buyer beware. There's a helpful principle summed up in these insightful words of Jesus: "If you don't believe me when I tell you about earthly things, how can you possibly believe if I tell you about heavenly things?"[9]

For example, Mormon teachings (and thus, Mormon authority) suffer under this first test. Their writings and teachers make clear claims about entire civilizations that were supposed to have lived in the ancient Americas. The details about these peoples were purportedly written on golden tablets that were translated by Joseph Smith in the early 1800s. But you can't see or test the golden tablets because, according to the story, an angel "whisked them away" after Smith was done with them.

You also can't verify anything about these ancient civilizations because historians have discovered no evidence that they ever existed. Furthermore, the Smithsonian Institution sends out a form letter to anyone who inquires saying, "The Book of Mormon is a religious document and not a scientific guide. The Smithsonian Institution has never used it in archeological research, and any information that you have received to the contrary is incorrect." In an earlier form of the same letter, which they sent out for years, titled "Statement Regarding the Book of Mormon," they forthrightly declared: "Smithsonian archeologists see no direct connection between the archeology of the New World and the subject matter of the book." And finally, a recent study showed conclusive DNA evidence that the Native American people on the North American continent share no genetic links with the Israelites or any other Middle Eastern people group, contradicting the clear claims in the Book of Mormon that these so-called Lamanites were of Hebrew de-

True to their own words *means that leaders must not only be honest and consistent, but they must also prove to be right about things they declare to be true.*

scent. On the contrary, the DNA studies showed that these people were actually descended from Asian ancestors.[10]

I know these are hard facts for our Mormon friends to hear, but if their books and prophets can't be verified in regard to these "earthly things," it ought to give them strong pause about believing their books and prophets when they talk about unseen spiritual things. The principle of *accuracy* is one we all must be willing to apply as we test the teachings of would-be spiritual authorities in our own lives, including any writings that claim to be scriptural.

True to their own words means that the leaders must not only be honest and consistent, as we've said, but they must also prove to be right about things they declare to be true. For example, when a pastor with a healing ministry proclaims that a person "has been healed of polio," that person had better have had the symptoms in the first place and then be truly free of those symptoms tonight, tomorrow, and six months from now. Otherwise, the words—and the credibility—of that teacher prove empty.

When someone declares "in the name of the Lord" that a specific event is about to happen, yet that event fails to materialize, your trust in that "prophet" or alleged representative of God ought to fail to materialize as well. Look at these powerful words of warning from the Hebrew prophet Moses:

> But you may wonder, "How will we know whether or not a prophecy is from the LORD?" If the prophet speaks in the LORD's name but his prediction does not happen or come true, you will know that the LORD did not give that message. That prophet has spoken without my authority and need not be feared.[11]

This is a warning worth heeding in regard to any message that claims to be prophetic. For example, if you are considering the teachings of the Jehovah's Witnesses, you should be aware that their "prophets" have made repeated false predictions about the return of Christ throughout the movement's history. According to their earliest teachers, the Battle of Armageddon and the destruction of all world powers would happen in 1914. When that didn't happen, they reinterpreted the prophecy and put out a new edition—it would all happen in 1918. Oops! Well, it would occur by 1925 for sure. This pattern of revising and updating went on repeatedly throughout the twentieth century, including more recent predictions for 1975.[12] Not only that, but one of their clearest and boldest prophecies, which was printed

on the front of every *Alive* magazine until recent years, proclaimed that we would see fulfillment of "the Creator's promise of a peaceful and secure new world before the generation that saw the events of 1914 passes away." Needless to say, the clock is quickly running out on that prophecy as well.

True to God's words *means that the doctrines espoused must square with the teachings of any real revelation or true scriptures from God.*

Before choosing your faith, you owe it to yourself to make sure that the leaders of the faith movement under consideration are true to their own words—especially when they are supposed to be speaking words from God on which you will stake your life.

True to God's words means that the doctrines espoused must square with the teachings of any real revelation or true scriptures from God. Now, I've not hidden the fact that I think there is a collection of writings that gives evidence of being both true and inspired by God—and I would want any leader I chose to follow to be faithful to that God and his book as the ultimate authorities. But I don't want to get too far ahead of myself; in a later chapter, I'll present some of the reasons why I've concluded that the Bible is genuinely the Word of God—and that it's the best guide we have available to help us discern which, if any, faith to finally choose.

Openness

One more test of authority will suffice for now. The leader or organization must not resist scrutiny or questioning of their integrity, consistency, and accuracy. *Openness* is an important component of integrity. True integrity has nothing to hide. Likewise, openness is necessary for evaluating consistency. How can you really know whether a person's integrity goes all the way to the depths of who they are if they're not open about it? So, a spiritual leader shouldn't mind living as an open book.

Earlier, we noted that Jesus invited his critics to examine his life and uncover any shortcomings. The apostle Paul reflected this same kind of openness by the way he lived out his values amid the people he taught and led: "You know of our concern for you from the way we lived when we were with you. . . . Keep putting into practice all you learned and received from me—everything you heard from me and saw me doing. Then the God of peace will be with you."[13]

It might go without saying, but the kind of openness and humility I'm talking about are often not exhibited by religious leaders and organizations—across the spectrum (I'm not singling out any particular one). Many are secretive, covering up their mistakes and hiding blunders and sins of the past—as well as concealing their sketchy financial practices of the present. They might put on a positive exterior, but when you start to ask too many questions or probe too deeply, that surface-level niceness can quickly disappear as their defenses go up. Some even become hostile and threaten challengers with litigation or physical harm. Whether their resistance is extreme and overt or a more benign neglect of your questions and your desire to test their authority, if you're finding a persistent lack of openness, red flags should go up in your mind. You should proceed with extreme caution, if at all. Authorities worth following—competent and confident ones—are not afraid of questions, and they don't have to apply intimidation or wield fear to gain a following.

As you examine the spiritual authorities and influences in your life and put them to the test, I believe it will help you move toward finding a worthwhile and trustworthy faith.

As you examine the spiritual authorities and influences in your life and put them to the test using the criteria listed above, I believe it will help you move toward finding a worthwhile and trustworthy faith—one with credentials you can count on.

∞

My friend Nabeel grew up in an Islamic family, whose members he describes as being among the most dedicated Muslims he has ever known. Although born a U.S. citizen, he was taught to read the Quran in Arabic by the age of four, and he had read the entire book—and even memorized whole chapters of it—by the time he was five. As a young boy, he was often held up as a model for other children in the local Islamic community. He grew up studying the Quran, offering prayers five times a day, and living for Allah in the most devoted way he knew how. Islam was not just his religion; it was his blueprint for life.

Then, in college, he became friends with David, who turned out to be a committed Christian. When Nabeel saw David reading his Bible one evening, he immediately challenged him, insisting that no reasonable person could trust the Christian scriptures. This led to a series of lively and impassioned discussions that spanned over the next several years. They talked about some of the same issues I had raised with the imam in the mosque several years earlier: did Jesus really claim to be the Son of God, was he crucified on a cross, and (probably the most important question) did he really rise from the dead?

Much to Nabeel's surprise, David offered strong logic and evidence for his beliefs. In fact, the deeper Nabeel looked and the harder he studied, the more he became convinced that David's answers made sense. This shook his confidence in the authority of the Muslim faith, so he asked Allah to give him reassurance through answers to specific prayers and through dreams or visions. Those prayers were answered in uncanny ways—but not in the ways he had expected. Rather, they pointed him again and again toward the faith David was presenting and away from the teachings of Islam.

Frustrated and nearly desperate, Nabeel decided to put what he was discovering to the test by consulting some experts who might help him. He traveled to Washington, D.C., Canada, and England in search of knowledgeable Muslims who might answer David's arguments against Islam. In the process, he heard a variety of responses, which, as he put it later, "ran the gamut from terribly unconvincing to fairly innovative," and he encountered people who "ranged from sincere to condescendingly caustic." At the end of his research, the arguments for and against Islam still hung in the balance, but one thing had become abundantly clear in his mind: those arguments were far from approaching the strength of the case for Christianity.

Finally, after years of searching, and contrary to the spiritual authority that had been over his life since childhood, he chose his faith. It was in Jesus as the Son of God, who, Nabeel had come to believe, had died and truly risen to become the Savior of the world.

You may or may not agree with Nabeel's conclusion. But don't you admire his courage and his willingness to seek the truth and follow the evidence wherever it led him, even when that journey became uncomfortable?

I think you'll also be encouraged by his words to fellow seekers about searching for the true God:

I invite you to search for Him and lay your current life on the line as I did. He is there, and He is waiting for you to come to Him so that He can walk with you. . . . But be sure that you really are ready for your life to change; I guarantee you, it will. . . . My prayers are with you.[14]

CHAPTER FIVE

"I JUST *FEEL* THAT IT'S TRUE"

Intuition and Knowledge

It was a classic *Star Wars* movie moment.

Obi-Wan Kenobi, the Jedi Master, was training Luke Skywalker, his young apprentice, on how to effectively use his lightsaber in battle. But after a few failed attempts by Luke to hit a small, rapidly flying "seeker" robot, Obi-Wan decided it was time to instill some new insights into his student.

"I suggest you try it again, Luke," he said, as he placed a large helmet over Luke's head, including a blast shield that completely covered his eyes. "This time, let go of your conscious self and act on instinct. . . . Your eyes can deceive you. Don't trust them."

Obi-Wan then threw the seeker into the air. It dropped straight down, and as Luke swung at it blindly and missed, it fired out a laser bolt that hit Luke right in the seat of his pants. Luke let out a yelp as he swung wildly once more, trying in vain to hit the seeker with his lightsaber.

"Stretch out with your feelings," Obi-Wan advised him.

Doing his best to apply the lesson, Luke stood in one place, seemingly frozen. The seeker made another dive at him, and this time—surprisingly—he managed to deflect the laser bolt.

"You see, you can do it," Obi-Wan encouraged.

"You know," Luke said to Obi-Wan, "I did feel something. I could almost see the remote."

"That's good," Obi-Wan replied. "You have taken your first step into a larger world."[1]

∞

This scene from Star Wars offers a pretty good picture of how some people try to assess their spiritual options: They turn off their senses, ignore their logic, and just *feel* their way into whatever belief or practice seems right to them.

This is especially true for people whose beliefs are influenced by Eastern religions in which the physical world and sensory experience are viewed as maya, or illusion, and truth is seen not as logical but as intuitive. "Stretch out with your feelings," Obi-Wan coached Luke. It was an approach based on the Buddhist-oriented philosophy of George Lucas, the writer and creative genius behind *Star Wars*.

In a *Time* interview with Bill Moyers, Lucas talked about the importance of taking a leap of faith: "You'll notice Luke uses that quite a bit through the film—not to rely on pure logic, not to rely on the computers, but to rely on faith. That is what that 'Use the Force' is: a leap of faith. There are mysteries and powers larger than we are, and you have to trust your feelings in order to access them."[2]

According to this approach, which I'll refer to as the *Intuitive* faith path, real perception resides in feelings and instinct. That's where you'll find the most reliable sense of direction, though it will often be gained in hidden places and be easily overlooked by the masses of people—who are caught up in the world of sights and sounds, and who are missing the deeper, esoteric realities only available to those who search them out using their innate sixth sense.

Here's how some people try to assess their spiritual options: They turn off their senses, ignore their logic, and just feel *their way into whatever belief or practice seems right to them.*

That's why Transcendental Meditation (TM) practitioners instruct their inductees to relax their minds, empty themselves of all conscious thought, and open up to what they promise will be an internal sense of peace and wholeness (along with, many would argue, a whole raft of Hindu ideas). The founder of the Transcendental Meditation methodology, Maharishi Mahesh Yogi, said this during a talk he gave in Switzerland:

> With Transcendental Meditation, the activity of the mind settles down, and when the activity of the mind settles down, the

> mind is in the character of unbounded awareness. . . . It's like
> a wave in the ocean . . . settling down . . . unbounded quiet
> level of the water. So Transcendental Meditation creates this
> transcendental consciousness.[3]

Another philosopher who taught along these same lines, until his death in 1986, was Dr. J. Krishnamurti of Oxford, England, who "located the human problem in our thoughts, a result of conditioning received during our lives as humans as we passed through various stages of intellectual development. He advocated 'freedom from thoughts' as the means of liberation."[4]

∞

These views are not limited to the world of movies or to Eastern meditation and mantras. Many New Age–oriented success teachers and writers will also coach you to stop trying to think and reason your way through life and to instead let your inner voice guide you in the ways you should go.

Napoleon Hill's 1937 classic, *Think and Grow Rich*, has been called the granddaddy of all motivational literature and has sold more than 30 million copies worldwide. Hill's ideas have influenced generations of business leaders and success seekers, as well as an entire industry of self-help books. In light of that sweeping impact, it's interesting to get his take on the subject of learning and choosing our beliefs:

> Throughout history, people have depended too much upon
> their physical senses and have limited their knowledge to
> physical things they could see, touch, weigh, and measure. We
> are now entering the most marvelous of all ages—an age which

will teach us something of the intangible forces of the world about us. Perhaps we shall learn as we pass through this age, that the "other self" is more powerful than the physical self we see when we look in a mirror.[5]

In a later chapter, with the spiritual-sounding title "The Sixth Sense: The Door to the Temple of Wisdom," Hill adds these thoughts:

Somewhere in the cell structure of the human brain is an area which receives vibrations of thought ordinarily called hunches. So far, science has not discovered where this site of the Sixth Sense is located, but this is not important. The fact remains that human beings do receive accurate knowledge, through sources other than the five physical senses. . . .

Nearly all great leaders, such as Napoleon, Bismarck, Joan of Arc, Christ, Buddha, Confucius, and Mohammed, understood and made use of the Sixth Sense almost continuously. The major portion of their greatness consisted of their knowledge of this principle.

The sixth sense is not something that one can take off and put on at will. Ability to use this great power comes slowly.[6]

This intuitive approach to feeling one's way into a particular set of beliefs, or to a faith, has been around for a long time, but it is growing in popularity and appeal, in part because of people like Napoleon Hill and others who have been similarly influential. But there is also an inherent factor of intrigue at play. The idea of knowing things that others don't know, through internal and hidden processes, has a certain mystique and appeal. It also seems to sidestep the need for rigorous thought, study, investigation—or even accountability—opting instead for more direct and private forms of enlightenment and understanding.

The promise is also made that if you properly apply and focus your mental energy, it will bring great rewards. One of the current best-selling books is *The Secret*, by Rhonda Byrne, which picks up and expands on many of these ideas. Here's what Byrne says about the Intuitive approach, echoing some of Napoleon Hill's thoughts and mixing in a bit more of the mystical as well:

The idea of knowing things that others don't know, through internal and hidden processes, has a certain mystique and appeal.

Trust your instincts. It's the Universe inspiring you. It's the Universe communicating with you on the receiving frequency. If you have an intuitive or instinctive feeling, follow it, and you will find that the Universe is magnetically moving you to receive what you asked for. . . .

Remember that you are a magnet, attracting everything to you. When you have gotten clear in your mind about what you want, you have become a magnet to draw those things to you, and those things you want are magnetized to you in return. The more you practice and begin to see the law of attraction bringing things to you, the greater the magnet you will become, because you will add the power of faith, belief, and knowing.[7]

∞

Even in leadership circles and popular business books, it sometimes sounds like intuition is winning over information as the way to make the quickest and most reliable decisions. That's how some people interpret the popular book *Blink: The Power of Thinking Without Thinking*, by best-selling author Malcolm Gladwell. In the opening pages, Gladwell begins with a story of "The Statue That Didn't Look Right":

> In September of 1983, an art dealer by the name of Gianfranco Becchina approached the J. Paul Getty Museum in California. He had in his possession, he said, a marble statue dating from the sixth century BC. It was what is known as a kouros—a sculpture of a nude male youth standing with his left leg forward and his arms at his sides. There are only about two hundred kouroi in existence, and most have been recovered badly damaged or in fragments from grave sites or archeological digs. But this one was almost perfectly preserved. It stood close to seven feet tall. It had a kind of light-colored glow that set it apart from other ancient works. It was an extraordinary find. Becchina's asking price was just under $10 million.[8]

The people at the Getty proceeded carefully. They took the Greek statue on loan, and then they went to work studying it and all of the documentation that came with it in order to determine for certain if it was authentic. They analyzed core samples of the artifact using an electron microscope, electron microprobe, mass spectrometry, X-ray diffraction, and X-ray fluorescence, and they studied the layer of calcite on the surface of the statue, which appeared to be hundreds or even thousands of years old.[9]

After more than a year of critically examining this statue in every way they could dream up, they were finally satisfied and decided to make the grand purchase. In 1986, they put the celebrated sculpture on public display. This created so much excitement that the story made the front page of the *New York Times*.

But something wasn't right. As top art experts and historians saw the kouros in person, they candidly commented on how it just didn't look the way it should. It was hard for them to put a finger on the exact issue, but they sensed there was a problem. One world-class authority on Greek sculpture instinctively knew immediately upon seeing it that something was wrong. She just had "a hunch, an instinctive sense that something was amiss."[10]

When Thomas Hoving, former director of the Metropolitan Museum of Art, saw the statue, the first word that came to his mind was *fresh*. "And 'fresh,'" he said, "was not the right reaction to have to a two-thousand-year-old statue. . . . The kouros looked like it had been dipped in the very best caffè latte from Starbucks."[11] He told the museum curator that the Getty should not buy it; or if they already had, that they should try to get their money back. Another expert, this one from Greece, saw the statue and "immediately felt cold." He quickly determined that the work was a fake because when he first laid his eyes on it, he felt a wave of what he described as "intuitive repulsion."[12]

Gladwell sums up the situation: "The Getty, with its lawyers and scientists and months of painstaking investigation, had come to one conclusion, and some of the world's foremost experts in Greek sculpture—just by looking at the statue and sensing their own 'intuitive repulsion'—had come to another. Who was right?"[13]

I'll bet you can instinctively guess who was right. It turned out that the sculpture was in fact a forgery, and the intuitive experts had been vindicated. "In the first two seconds of look-ing—in a single glance—they were able to understand more about the essence of the statue than the team at the Getty was able to understand after fourteen months."[14]

∞

So, in light of the avalanche of illustrations and examples of the power of intuition, why not just go with it? Why not feel our way through our daily decisions, including deciding what to believe about the spiritual realm?

That was the approach of a woman who worked at a gift shop in La Jolla, California. When Heidi, my wife, made a passing comment to her with a spiri-tual theme, this lady was quick to speak up about her strong faith. As we talked with her, we discovered it was a faith in a variety of New Age ideas, includ-ing the power of horoscopes and the insights of fortune-tellers. Her deeply held beliefs also included a "Jesus" who was very close to her, who would never tell anyone they were wrong or judge them for their actions or religious posi-tion, and who seemed to be completely and coincidentally aligned with her own

So, why not just go with it? Why not feel our way through our daily decisions, including deciding what to believe about the spiritual realm?

views on all these things. When I tried to gently raise the issue of what Jesus actually taught about some of these topics, she bristled. "My Jesus isn't like that," she said emphatically. How did she know? Because she could feel it in her heart.

Well, before we discuss some problems with this approach to choosing one's beliefs and faith, let me first acknowledge a few things.

First, it's hard to argue with the fact that we truly are, as the Hebrew scriptures put it, "fearfully and wonderfully made."[15] (Even if you're a complete naturalist, won't you at least admit that we are, at minimum, "fearfully and wonderfully evolved" in ways you can't fully explain in purely naturalistic terms?) As amazingly complex *Homo sapiens*, we should not be surprised that we have some level of built-in intuitive instinct that works with our other senses—and perhaps sometimes even independently—to give us quick and clear impressions of dangers, opportunities, or direction. We know many animals have these instincts in various forms, so why not we humans, too?

In fact, we often talk in terms of instinct. It's widely accepted, for example, that females of our species generally have a higher awareness of extra-sensory understanding. We call it "woman's intuition."

Anyone who knows Heidi would observe that she dwarfs me with her sense of intuition. I tend to be more of a "knowledge person," who studies facts and information, often taking things at face value. "He seems like an honest guy," I'll tell Heidi, "and the product seems like a good one. So I think we should buy from him." To which she replies, "I can see why you'd say that," (translation: *People like you, who lack the requisite radar, tend to fall for things like this.*) "but I sense that something's not right about this man and what he's telling us. I think we should keep looking around before we make any purchases." I've been married to Heidi long enough, and have been tutored by past experience often enough, to have learned that I neglect her discernment only at great risk. She pretty much always turns out to be right.

On a broader level, we also understand that certain people, male and female, have a more developed sense of awareness and insight, being able to read a room, an audience, or an individual—sometimes even at great distances. For example, they do it just by hearing a person's voice on the phone or by merely looking at someone's handwriting.

In religious circles, as well, we acknowledge that certain members of a congregation have unusual gifts of wisdom or discernment. The general understanding of those "spiritual gifts" is not that these people typically hear God's voice in a direct way, but that their spiritual sensitivity is more highly

In religious circles, we acknowledge that certain members have unusual gifts of wisdom or discernment. Their spiritual sensitivity is more highly refined.

refined, and thus they are more attuned to what is happening at deeper levels than normal observation would reveal. Whether this level of awareness is the person's routine way of functioning or only comes in occasional flashes of insight, it can be very important for the group in making decisions or avoiding danger.

∞

I have a friend who called his travel agent to book a cross-country business trip. She advised him on the best flight to take to get to his destination, and upon gaining his approval, was in the process of typing in his reservation. As he heard her keying in the information, he suddenly felt that he ought to ask her on what airline she was booking him. As soon as she told him which carrier it was, he surprised her—and probably himself, too—when he blurted out, "I don't feel comfortable with that. What are my other options?"

She studied her computer screen for a moment and then said with some hesitation, "Well, you could fly a different airline into another nearby city, but it would be a significant number of miles from where you're trying to get to. You'd have to rent a car and drive a lot farther. I'm sure you wouldn't want to do that."

He again responded in an unexpected way: "Yes, that's what I'd like to do. Go ahead and book me into the other city." She complied with his request, though she was probably shaking her head at his insistence on going so far out of his way, and booked him on the alternative flight.

A few weeks later, my friend boarded his airplane, which took off within ten minutes of the more convenient flight he had opted not to take. About ninety minutes later, he landed safely, had dinner at a restaurant near the airport, and got into his rental car for the long drive to his destination. That's when he turned on the radio—and heard the shocking news that the other flight had flipped over in the air and crashed as it was nearing the airport, killing everyone on board.

∞

How did my friend know that he needed to switch flights? It's a great question, but the truth is that he really didn't *know*. If you asked him why he made that abrupt decision on the phone with the travel agent, he wouldn't tell you he heard an audible directive from heaven or even a quiet spiritual voice talking to him. He simply felt that he needed to go on the other flight. He trusted his instinct and is alive today to talk about it.

It's also worth adding that we all have an inward sense of moral intuition, what we call our con-science, that guides us regarding what's right and wrong (unless we ignore or abuse it until it's beyond repair). This internal "ethical compass" gives us a sense of direction about decisions and standards we should live by—but most of the time we would understand it to be a natural (even if God-given) phe-nomenon, not a special revelation from a divine source.

We all have an inward sense of moral intuition, what we call our conscience, that guides us regarding what's right and wrong.

It is interesting, too, that spiritual leaders in biblical times sometimes made decisions based on a merely intuitive sense. The apostle Paul, for example, after arriving at a certain town where he wanted to minister, said, "I had no peace of mind because my dear brother Titus hadn't yet arrived with a report from you. So I said good-bye and went on to Macedonia to find him."[16] At least in this case there was no divine voice, no angelic guidance, no prophetic word—just a guy who lacked peace, followed his feelings, and made what seemed at the time to be a wise decision.

∞

If there is a God who is wise, powerful, and full of knowl-edge, then it certainly follows that he would be able to give us data that goes beyond the normal information available to us through our senses. This could be accomplished in the form of unconscious guidance that helps us, coming into our awareness beneath the usual sensory radar. We may not know where it emanates from, but it can help us in very important ways.

So, from many different sources of understanding and experience, we see that we are endowed with instincts and insights that can make enormous differences in our lives. Blaise Pascal said famously, *"Le coeur a ses raisons que la raison ne connaît point."* "The heart has its reasons of which reason knows nothing."[17] When we need to size up a person or evaluate a situation, we're always wise to consult our heart—or, as it's sometimes crassly stated in the business world, we should "do a gut check." Combined with gaining input from friends or coworkers who have deeper levels of wisdom and insight, this can save us a lot of heartache along the way.

But watch out. Many hearts have been broken—and lives shattered—by following the heart alone. Hunches, intuitive flashes, and "gut feelings" can serve as cautionary alerts—but whenever possible, these need to be tested against other proven methods of finding and affirming truth. In other words, they can be great warning lights, but in isolation, they're generally not great traffic signals to direct us.

∞

To illustrate the limited nature of intuitive information, let's look back through some of our examples, starting with the scene from *Star Wars*. Remember that Obi-Wan Kenobi put the helmet on Luke Skywalker and told him to skip using his eyes and just act on instinct. But notice that Obi-Wan failed to heed his own advice. That is, he did not put on his helmet to block his own sight in order to instinctively sense how Luke was doing with this new, superior approach. Instead, he stood and observed him in the old-fashioned way—with his own two eyes—which were just like the ones he had told Luke not to be deceived by. So much for stretching out with your feelings.

And what are we to make of the Transcendental Meditation advice that says we all need to empty our minds and think about nothing? First, we have to wonder if it's really even possible. I mean, how would we *know* that we were actually thinking about nothing without harboring in our minds the thought, *I'm finally thinking about nothing?* You see, in that case we'd actually be *thinking about* thinking about nothing, which is a thought in itself—one that would disqualify us at that very moment from thinking about nothing.

I also agree with this incisive critique I read recently:

The guru who tells us that our thoughts are the problem has reached this conclusion and communicated it to us only by use of the very faculties that he decries. We are caught in a web of contradiction from which there is no escape. In fact, the logical conclusion of this philosophy is total silence—absence of communication. An ancient Indian scripture called the *Kenopanishad* has this unaffirmable quote: "He who speaks does not know, and he who knows does not speak."[18]

In many ways, this approach seems self-contradictory and self-defeating and therefore eliminates itself as being a viable option, as we'll see more fully in a later chapter on logic.

And what of Napoleon Hill and his bold assertion that we were entering the age of hunches and reliance on our sixth sense? It's interesting that his conclusions throughout *Think and Grow Rich* were drawn from a lifetime of study and observation. In fact, the title page of the book affirms that it was "organized through 25 years of research, in collaboration with more than 500 distinguished men of great wealth, who proved by their achievements that this philosophy is practical." In other words, Hill didn't get the bulk of his information from instinct, hunches, or sixth-sense insights. He got it the old-fashioned way, by working hard, observing carefully, and then logically laying out what he'd learned. He was perhaps aided by intuition and instinct (and also, it could be argued, a fair amount of speculation and mysticism), but it certainly was not in isolation from these other vital elements of learning.

Their hunches were informed hunches, and these were supported and tested in their own minds by broader bits of evidence and information.

And think back to the story of the Greek statue. Who were those people who had the correct initial "blink" reactions? They weren't just highly intuitive people pulled in off the street. No, they were specialists experienced in the study of ancient sculptures and artifacts. In other words, they were knowledgeable men and women with trained instincts. Their hunches were *informed* hunches, and these were supported and tested in their own minds by broader bits of evidence and information. And even after these world-class experts experienced their "intuitive repulsions" and communicated their concerns about the statue, the Getty people still did extensive research—of the traditional, scientific kind—to test and verify the feedback.

Malcolm Gladwell recognizes the limitations of intuition

and even offers a caveat in the introduction to his book: "*Blink* is not just a celebration of the power of the glance, however. I'm also interested in those moments when our instincts betray us. . . . When should we trust our instincts, and when should we be wary of them? . . . When our powers of rapid cognition go awry, they go awry for a very specific and consistent set of reasons, and those reasons can be identified and understood. . . . The third and most important task of this book is to convince you that our snap judgments and first impressions can be educated and controlled."[19] Gladwell spends the latter part of the book qualifying the use of initial impressions and teaching readers how to train, inform, and guide their intuitive sense.

And what about the feeling my friend had that he needed to book the other flight for his business trip? Well, he told me later that he was aware at the time that the airline he was almost booked on had struggled with safety issues in recent years. So, that knowledge was likely influencing him, even if not overtly. It's also possible, and I think very likely, that there was some unseen divine intervention protecting and guiding him, though below the level of consciousness. So, there's no need to conclude that this was merely an unguided intuitive sense. Rather, it was likely a confluence of his own thoughts and impressions based on relevant data and information, along with instincts and perhaps supernatural protection.

It's also worth noting that, generally speaking, even the most ardent promoters of the Intuitive approach usually ignore that approach when it comes to everyday living. That's why they drive down the highway with their eyes wide open (not wearing helmets with blast shields, thankfully), check the expiration dates on food before they buy it, study the financial health of businesses before they invest in their stock, and get advanced degrees in various areas of study—none of which seems to model the purported priority of intuitive knowledge.

It's also interesting that those who advocate the intuitive way of knowing routinely write detailed logical defenses of it, trying to support it by using evidence and examples drawn from daily life. They don't tell you just to clutch their books to your heart or hold them over your head as you decide through some sixth sense if what they are saying is true. Rather, they give you *reasons* to trust them, buy their books, and listen to their lectures—reasons why you should then ignore reason and just go with your intuition.

∞

Let me conclude by asking, if intuition provides a warning light or a sense of direction that should be tested and affirmed by other means, why would anyone base their faith—as well as their life and eternity—solely on hunches, feelings, or impressions? Intuition is, at best, an imperfect guide. We tend to forget all the times it was wrong and selectively remember the times—however rare—when it was actually right.

And what about psychics and others who claim to have special access to the mysteries of truth and knowledge? If they really had the intuitive information they claim to have, they wouldn't be sitting around in shoddy little booths reading sweaty palms for paltry sums of money. They'd be rich from playing the lottery and the stock market because they'd know exactly when to buy their tickets and where to lay down their investments. Their lack of success betrays their lack of insight.

I should also point out that the writers of the Bible caution us to be suspicious of our own independent assessments. Solomon, for example, considered by many to be the wisest man who ever lived, warned ominously in the book of Proverbs, "There is a path before each person that seems right, but it ends in death."[20] Add to that the writings of the prophet Jeremiah: "The human heart is the most deceitful of all things, and desperately wicked."[21] That's a hard indictment to hear, but if you look through the window of history or into the mirror of your own life, it's also hard to refute.

Even the most ardent promoters of the Intuitive approach usually ignore that approach when it comes to everyday living. That's why they drive down the highway with their eyes wide open.

We need to pay attention to our instincts, but we also need to scrutinize and corroborate them carefully. We must test what we *sense* to be true against logic and evidence. If we claim to follow Jesus, as the woman in La Jolla said she did, we must honestly assess what we think we know against Jesus' real teachings. Don't let Napoleon Hill, a New Age book or seminar, or your inner voice tell you what Jesus taught and meant. Don't go by what you *imagine* or *wish* he had said; instead, look at what he actually did say. In other words, let him speak for himself. He's the one who declared, "My sheep listen to my voice; I know them, and they follow me."[22]

As you test your intuition and insights, you'll be that much closer to wisely choosing your faith.

CHAPTER SIX

"GOD *TOLD* ME IT'S TRUE!"

The Mystical Approach

"I've read the *Book of Mormon,* and I prayed and asked the Heavenly Father to show me if it was true—as it tells us to do in Moroni chapter 10—and God clearly answered my prayers," a sweet teenager named Rachael said earnestly to me and others sitting around the table.[1]

"I can tell you with all my heart that I know this book is true," she continued, her voice trembling and tears welling in her eyes as she clutched the

Mormon scriptures. "And if you'll just pray and ask the Father the way I did, he'll show you the same thing. This book is so precious to me, and I love God so much—I just want everybody to know this too. . . ." Her voice trailed off as she was overwhelmed with emotion.

It was a tender, though admittedly awkward, moment. No one could doubt Rachael's sincerity, nor did anyone want to venture a differing opinion, out of respect for her and the heartfelt testimony she'd just given.

∞

Let's face it: Claims of mystical encounters with supernatural beings—whether spirits, angels, departed loved ones, or even God himself—are difficult (if not impossible) to prove or disprove. Frankly, they're simply hard to argue with. Even if you're not convinced that the implications of the reported experience are true, it's natural to think, *Who am I to tell this girl that many people believe the* Book of Mormon *is fraught with inconsistencies, or that her church has been accused of having a very shaky foundation of unsupported speculation and stories?*

So, how can we deal with these kinds of accounts? Let's back up and examine this approach of choosing one's faith, which I'm calling the *Mystical* faith path. This one goes beyond the intuitive method we discussed in chapter 5 because it entails not just a human instinct or some kind of natural "sixth sense" that leads a person to certain beliefs; rather, the Mystical method bases its position on claims of an actual encounter with a supernatural entity. And because this path tends to be more spiritual in nature, you'll see that some of the ways we can test it are also of a more spiritual nature.

Here's an initial observation: Not all mystical claims are created equal. For example, consider the man I met years ago in Orange County, California, who confided that he was one of the two prophets described in the last book of the Bible and predicted to appear sometime near the end of the world.[2] I wondered what I had done to make myself worthy of such an astounding disclosure—and was surprised that a person of such importance would be hanging out in a shabby sandwich shop in downtown Santa Ana.

That experience was strange, but not quite as odd as my encounter with someone to whom I gave a ride from a music festival. (I know you're not supposed to pick up hitchhikers, but he knew some of my friends and seemed normal enough—at least at first.) Things started getting weird about midway through our journey. I don't know whether he viewed me as trustworthy, gullible, or both, but he decided to let me in on a cosmic secret: *He was the Holy Spirit!*

Claims of mystical encounters with supernatural beings— whether spirits, angels, departed loved ones, or even God himself—are difficult (if not impossible) to prove or disprove.

Well, to be fair, he actually claimed that his title was "The Comforter," based on Jesus' description of the Holy Spirit in John 16. Needless to say, I was a bit taken aback by this assertion, especially when he went on to affirm that he had been present during the events described in the first chapter of Genesis—and had, in fact, participated in the creation of the world. Now, I've never claimed to fully grasp all of the intricacies of the

Christian doctrine of the Trinity, but I was pretty sure that "The Comforter" sitting in the passenger seat of my car wasn't part of it.

Or there was the time when I was helping an elderly couple in the stereo store where I worked, and the woman decided to broach a spiritual discussion. When she saw I was open to talking about the topic, she decided to venture a step further. "God did a wonderful miracle in my husband's life many years ago," she said. "Can we tell you about it?"

"Sure," I said, always interested in spiritual matters. With that, her husband, who had been silent up until that point,

How can we sort out any real facts from fiction? When we start choosing our faith based on mystical feelings or encounters, it becomes supremely important.

could not contain his pent-up enthusiasm. "A number of years ago, I died," he exclaimed in excited tones, "and God worked through a wonderful prophet, who prayed over my body and raised me back to life again."

"Really?" I asked, sensing the sincerity of their claim while trying to hide the incredulity in my mind. "That's amazing."

Maybe you've encountered these kinds of stories in your own life. Perhaps a friend has passed along a similar account, or you've seen incredible claims on the Internet. They tell you about someone they know (actually, it's more often a friend of a friend—or was it the friend's uncle?) who had an incredible experience. A man these people picked up and gave a ride to had warned them about the imminent end of the world, and then suddenly—*poof*—he disappeared. They can't remember the guy's name or the date it actually happened, but one thing's for sure: *It was an angel in their backseat.*

∞

What are we to make of these things? How can we sort out the real facts, if there are any, from fiction? It may not seem very important when it comes to rumors of angels riding in the backseat of who-knows-whose car on the back roads of Arkansas in the early 1970s, or of supposedly earthshaking events like scientists discovering hell in Siberia (did you hear about that one?). But when people like you or me, or young folks like Rachael, start choosing our faith based on mystical feelings or encounters, it becomes supremely important.

For starters, let me introduce the first of two important guidelines to help in evaluating mystical encounters:

Feel ≠ Real

I have no question that Rachael genuinely *felt* something when she prayed over her copy of the *Book of Mormon*. I'm far less confident about the end-times prophet in Santa Ana, the Comforter/Creator guy, or the man claiming to have been raised from the dead—though it's possible each was sincere in thinking he had felt or experienced something out of the ordinary. But what they *feel* does not necessarily equate with something that's *real*.

Let's look more deeply at Rachael's claim, which was touching in its presentation but predictable in its content. I've heard many Mormons give this same testimony over the years. Though it may reflect a sensation they actually felt, it's also part of their religious culture, their training, and the expectation among their members—and it is central to their evangelistic appeal.

One of the chief defenders of Mormonism today is Robert L. Millet, professor of ancient scripture and former dean of religious education at Brigham Young University. He wrote a book called *Getting at the Truth: Responding to Difficult Questions about LDS Beliefs*, which apparently is designed to be a training manual for members of the Mormon religion (officially called The Church of Jesus Christ of Latter-Day Saints—thus the "LDS" in the book title).

What follows are some examples of what Millet says about how to best choose one's faith, including several quotes from some highly placed Mormon leaders. Read these words carefully, because they provide a great example of the Mystical approach:

The most tried and true method of obtaining divine direction— [is] prayer itself.[3]

In a very real sense, believing is seeing. No member of the Church need feel embarrassed at being unable to produce the golden plates or the complete Egyptian papyrus. No member of the Church should hesitate to bear testimony of verities that remain in the realm of faith, that are seen only with the eyes of faith.[4]

President Ezra Taft Benson pointed out: "We do not have to prove the *Book of Mormon* is true. The book is its own proof. All we need to do is read it and declare it. . . . We are not required to prove that the *Book of Mormon* is true or is an authentic record through external evidences—though there are many. It never has been the case, nor is it so now, that the studies of the learned will prove the *Book of Mormon* true or false. The origin, preparation, translation, and verification of the truth of the *Book of Mormon* have all been retained in the hands of the Lord, and the Lord makes no mistakes. You can be assured of that."[5]

President Gordon B. Hinckley put things in proper perspective when he taught [regarding the *Book of Mormon*], . . . "The evidence for its truth, for its validity in a world that is prone to demand evidence, lies not in archaeology or anthropology, though these may be helpful to some. It lies not in word research or historical analysis, though these may be confirmatory. The evidence for its truth and validity lies within the covers of the book itself. The test of its truth lies in reading it. It is a book of God. Reasonable individuals may sincerely question its origin, but those who read it prayerfully may come to know by a power beyond their natural senses that it is true."[6]

Notice how this method of "knowing" truth is then turned into an approach for "showing" it to others:

Elder Boyd K. Packer declared, . . . "Do not be ill at ease or uncomfortable because you can give little more than your conviction. . . . If we can stand without shame, without hesitancy, without embarrassment, without reservation to bear witness that the gospel has been restored, that there are prophets and Apostles upon the earth, that the truth is available for all mankind, the Lord's Spirit will be with us. And that assurance can be affirmed to others."[7]

In the end, the only way that the things of God can be known is by the power of the Holy Ghost. . . . The only way spiritual truths may be known is by the quiet whisperings of the Holy Ghost.[8]

Then, near the close of this discussion, Millet attempts to assure his readers by giving his own testimony:

> I am grateful to have, burning within my soul, a testimony that the Father and the Son appeared to Joseph Smith in the Spring of 1820, and that The Church of Jesus Christ of Latter-Day Saints is truly the kingdom of God on earth.[9]

So, built on this mystical and experiential foundation, the strategy of the Mormon missionaries who come to your door is to give you some introductory information about their faith, including claims about their founder and prophet, Joseph Smith, his stories of early visions (yes, he built his beliefs on the Mystical approach, too), and the supposed origins of the *Book of Mormon*. Next, they'll testify to you about their own experience of having been assured by God concerning the truthfulness of all they've been taught and have now explained to you. Then they'll get to their real bottom line, which is to challenge you to do what they've done: to take the copy of the *Book of Mormon* that they will give you, read a portion of it, and then get on your knees and ask the Heavenly Father to show you if it's true.

The approach is simple, and it has proven very effective—Mormonism has for a long time been one of the faster-growing religious movements in the United States. So what, if anything, is wrong with the method?

Well, for one thing, the method is built on the assumption that *feel* must equal *real*. In other words, if you pray the way they ask you to, and then you feel anything remotely resembling a "burning in your soul," it supposedly means that everything they told you is true and that it's time for you to sign up to become a Mormon.

But let me venture some other possible explanations for why a person might *feel* something at this point.

First, it's important to realize that the type of people who accept this challenge to sit down and read the *Book of Mormon*, and then take time to pray to God—alone, unforced, unrehearsed, and unrelated to any church service or holiday meal with the family—are generally folks who haven't done these kinds of things in many years, if ever. So, they're already feeling more spiritual than usual, just because they're reading a faith-oriented book and doing religious-feeling activities. *There must be a God,* they think, *for someone like me to actually be taking this stuff seriously.*

If you accept a biblical view of things, you understand that there are real spiritual forces that oppose what is good—and they could be bringing a deceptive influence to bear.

And when they finally get down on their knees to pray, they naturally start to feel warm feelings—probably due to the simple fact that they are humbly bowing before their Maker. This might be the singular most saintly thing they've done in ten, twenty, or even thirty years. By this point, it is easy to imagine how these positive emotions could be misinterpreted to mean that the entire Mormon story is actually *true*.

Add to this the fact that as they read the *Book of Mormon*, some of it sounds familiar and seems to have a distinctive ring of truth. Why is that? It might be because whole chapters of it were copied almost word-for-word from the King James Version of the Bible. So if some of it sounds like "gospel truth," it's probably because parts of it actually are from the Gospels in the New Testament, and other portions are borrowed from the Old Testament.[10]

Also, if you accept a biblical view of things, you understand that there are real spiritual forces that oppose what is good—and they could be bringing a deceptive influence to bear.[11] We'll discuss this more later, but even the remote possibility of deception ought to give us pause before we assume that a burning sensation, a feeling of emotional warmth, or even the sense of a spiritual presence in the room automatically means that something is true, and we should join a particular religion.

That's probably why the Bible says to "test everything that is said. Hold on to what is good. Stay away from every kind of evil."[12] What's interesting about this admonition to "test everything" is that it comes immediately after the writer says, "Do not stifle the Holy Spirit. Do not scoff at prophecies."[13] So Paul, the author of the letter in question here, is not ruling out a mystical apprehension of truth; in fact, he's saying that we should stay open to things that God might want to say or do in our lives, even through powerful, mystical means. But we also must be very careful. Before we embrace new claims, we must test them against what we already know.

But how can we do this? One way is to apply the same triple test for accuracy that we discussed in chapter 4: Make sure that the message being given through the mystical encounter is (1) true to the world; (2) true to the messenger's own words; and, ultimately, (3) true to God's words.

First, and most obviously, if the new teachings are contrary to established facts in the world or claim a bunch of new ideas that aren't supported by known evidence, then warning alarms ought to be going off. Like the Mormon claims about entire civilizations, existing in the Americas, that are not supported by history, archaeology, or DNA testing.[14] Or the Muslim claim that Jesus never said he was the Son of God, didn't die on the cross, and therefore did not rise from the dead.[15] The historical record clearly tells us otherwise.

Second, we should look for internal inconsistencies to determine whether leaders or organizations are consistent with their own word. Examples in Mormonism, for instance, include the conflicting and contradictory accounts that Joseph Smith gave of his original vision; the unfulfilled prophecies he boldly declared as being the word of the Lord; hundreds of changes quietly made in later editions of the *Book of Mormon*—many of which radically changed the original meaning; and the Mormons' historical racism against dark-skinned people.[16] This racism was part of their doctrine all the way up until 1978 when, under public pressure, they received "new revelations" telling them to change their long-held prejudicial views and practices.[17] Similarly, the Watchtower Society, which is the leadership body over the Jehovah's Witnesses around the world, has characteristically played down, rationalized, or covered up their many false prophecies (including those we discussed in chapter 4).[18]

Third, a great model for testing spiritual encounters and teachings against God's words is seen in the early days of Christianity, when some new teachers who had come on the scene were still being scrutinized. One of those was Paul, who was a traveling teacher along with his colleague Silas. Listen to how one particular group of Christians responded: "And the people of Berea were more open-minded than those in Thessalonica, and they listened eagerly to Paul's message." They were open to what God might be trying to say to them through Paul's teaching, but they didn't exhibit blind receptivity. Instead, it says, "They searched the Scriptures day after day to see if Paul and Silas were teaching the truth."[19]

In effect, these people were saying, "We like what these guys are teaching—it all feels pretty good to us—but we're not going to take it on feelings alone. We're going to check it out. We'll test these claims of new truth against what we know to be established truth. Their message has to be true to God's words." So the Bereans tested the alleged new revelation from Paul against the known and trusted older revelation in the Hebrew scriptures.

"We like what these guys are teaching—it all feels pretty good to us—but we're not going to take it on feelings alone. We're going to check it out."

Another time, Paul taught this same principle himself: "But even if we or an angel from heaven should preach a gospel other than the one we preached to you, let him be eternally condemned! As we have already said, so now I say again: If anybody is preaching to you a gospel other than what you accepted, let him be eternally condemned."[20] Paul is telling his readers to test every teacher, *including Paul himself*, to carefully weigh what he and others said against what they knew to be true from the scriptures they already had (the Old Testament, the teachings of Jesus, and the writings and teachings of the other apostles). Even though Paul was an apostle himself, he says that we should not automatically trust someone just because he or she claims to be an apostle. Instead, we need to compare their message to the message that has already been received.

∞

Let's now apply this third test to our example of Mormonism and its Mystical approach to faith, keeping in mind that Mormons claim the Bible as part of their lineup of authoritative religious books. What we discover very quickly when we look in the Bible is that it does not teach a "pray and see if it feels right" methodology.[21] On the contrary, there's a strong scriptural principle that says, in effect, don't consider doing—and don't pray and ask God about—things he has already made it clear he's against.

For example, let's look at the story in the Gospel of Matthew when Jesus was fasting in the wilderness:

> The devil took [Jesus] to the holy city, Jerusalem, to the highest point of the Temple, and said, "If you are the Son of God, jump off! For the Scriptures say, 'He will order his angels to protect you. And they will hold you up with their hands so you won't even hurt your foot on a stone.'"
>
> Jesus responded, "The Scriptures also say, 'You must not test the LORD your God.'"[22]

This is a very interesting story, with the devil not only trying to tempt Jesus but quoting from the Bible to try to back up his position. Yet it was clear that he was tempting Jesus to do something that was out of God's will. So Jesus called him on it, warning the devil not to test the Lord.

Let me state this principle in contemporary terms. Let's say you recently bought a new sports car, and you're feeling tempted to see if it will really do the top speed the manufacturer claims it will. Or say that you're married, but you're feeling tempted to get romantically involved with someone at work who is not your spouse. Or your taxes are due, and you're going to owe more than you expected, so you're tempted to "adjust" the numbers to make the final amount a little more manageable.

In any of these three scenarios, can you imagine having the audacity of first praying to God and saying, "Dear Lord, just this once I want to drive 195 miles an hour on the highway; you'd be okay with that, wouldn't you?" or "Father, that new person at the office is so nice and . . . well . . . so good looking, a true testament to your divine creativity. So, would it be okay if we hooked up once or twice?" or "God, since the government is so wasteful of our tax money, would it be okay if this one time I tweaked the numbers on my return a bit, just to cut down on some of that governmental waste and put the money to better use?"

I certainly hope you wouldn't ask God to bless any of those plans. Because if you did, I think his response—if you were lucky and he was having a really good day—would be, at minimum, "Are you kidding me? Don't you already know what I've said about these things? You must not test the Lord your God!"

And yet I need to say—and this might surprise you—that when you understand the broader picture, the challenge to pray in order to determine whether Mormon teaching is correct is very similar to these examples. Let me explain how.

This is often not known by the general public, but Mormon teachings clearly assert that there are many gods—though we are to worship only one of those gods, the one who is over this world. That one god had a father and mother god, and each of them had parents, and so forth. Furthermore, Mormon theology affirms that every faithful Mormon man can become a god himself and someday be Lord over his own planet, producing with his wife (or wives) spirit children who will someday also become gods.

Joseph Smith, the founder of The Church of Jesus Christ of Latter-Day Saints, taught these things very clearly, as did the church's next leader, Brigham Young. In 1840, Lorenzo Snow, the church's fifth president, summed it up famously with a phrase that has been echoed in Mormon circles ever since: "As man is, God once was; as God is, man may become."[23]

Some Mormon teachers today seem to be distancing themselves from these classic teachings of their founders, prophets, and leaders. I find that some Mormons I talk to affirm and defend this doctrine, while others try to dodge it by saying, "I don't know anything about that." (I've actually gotten *both* of these responses within moments of each other during the same roundtable discussion—from two different Mormons. I said to the second one, the one who had just denied knowledge of the many gods doctrine, "Of course you know something about it—your friend here just defended it a few minutes ago.")

But even Mormon apologist Robert L. Millet, as recently as 2004, affirmed these doctrines when he wrote, "Latter-day scriptures state unequivocally that God is a man, a Man of Holiness (Moses 6:57), who possesses a body of flesh and bones (D&C 130:22). . . . What do we know beyond the truth that God is an exalted Man? What do we know of his mortal existence? What do we know of the time before he became God? Nothing. We really do not know more than what the Prophet Joseph Smith stated, and that is precious little."[24]

So, let me sum this up: In Mormonism, you have a belief in many gods, though only one of them is actually to be worshiped. This god is a changing being, who used to be a man but progressed over time toward godhood, just as faithful Mormon males will do.

But Mormonism is a faith that also claims to believe the Bible. The problem is that the Bible quite clearly challenges and refutes Mormon teachings. Here are a few examples:

> "I alone am God. There is no other God—there never has been, and there never will be. . . . You are witnesses that I am the only God," says the LORD. "From eternity to eternity I am God."[25]

> "For there is no other God but me, a righteous God and Savior. There is none but me. Let all the world look to me for salvation! For I am God; there is no other."[26]

> "I am the LORD, and I do not change."[27]

Now, as I affirmed in an earlier chapter, we need to be tolerant of others and support their right to believe and teach their religious points of view. But we also need to uphold our right to respectfully challenge those points of view—and, as lovers of truth, we should all be willing to do so.

Therefore, in light of the vastly contrasting message between the polytheistic (many gods) teachings of Mormonism and the monotheistic (one God) teachings of the Bible, I, for one, would reject the challenge to get on my knees and ask God if the Mormon faith is true.[28] I already know through the teachings of the Bible, which the Mormon faith purports to extend and expand, that Mormonism is not true. (And, as I'll explain in chapters 10 and 11, the Bible has the credentials to back up its own veracity.) Logic, therefore, tells me not to bother with praying to ask God about something that he has already made quite clear.

∞

Now let's look at a second guideline for how to examine mystical encounters:

Real ≠ Good

Even if the first test is passed and you become convinced that what you feel is actually real, the fact that it's real doesn't necessarily mean that it's good or from God.

Paul illustrated this principle in his letter to the church in Galatia, when he said, "But even if we *or an angel from heaven* should preach a gospel other than the one we preached to you, let him be eternally condemned!"[29] In other words, don't automatically put stock in a message you receive through a mystical experience—even if that experience is in the form of a real angelic being standing right in front of you—unless it passes the test by bringing a message consistent with what you already know to be true from God's previous revelation in the Bible.

We need to be tolerant of others and support their right to believe and teach their religious points of view. But we also need to uphold our right to respectfully challenge those points of view.

In another letter, Paul was explicit concerning why he gave these kinds of warnings: "Even Satan disguises himself as an angel of light. So it is no wonder that his servants also disguise themselves as servants of righteousness. In the end they will get the punishment their wicked deeds deserve."[30] The apostle John echoed these concerns when he wrote, "Dear friends, do not believe every spirit, but test the spirits to see whether they are from God, because many false prophets have gone out into the world."[31]

∞

This principle of Real ≠ Good played out for me years ago when I was teaching a class of a couple of hundred people, many of whom were in the process of deciding which faith to choose. I'd

Though much in the world of psychic phenomena, fortune-telling, and sorcery is mere intuition or deception, there are real supernatural powers and personalities that can work through these practices.

been warning about some of the errors of the so-called New Age movement, and that night I had focused on the deceptive and often dangerous practice of fortune-telling. I shared, based on evidence and firsthand studies, how most of what happens in fortune-telling is either fake or explainable through ordinary human perception and intuition (and sometimes through old-fashioned trickery). But then I added that it is possible that some psychics are aided with insights and knowledge from spiritual sources—*real* ones, but not *good* ones.

I finished my teaching and opened the floor for questions. To my surprise, a woman stood in the back of the room and announced that she was a professional psychic. Then she directed a challenge to me: "You can say anything you want about whether what I do is right or wrong, but I'm here to tell you that it works and that

I have insights that couldn't be discovered through any ordinary human means. It's a spiritual power, and it's real."

I took a deep breath and then thanked her for coming to the class and for reinforcing the last point I had made: Though much in the world of psychic phenomena, fortune-telling, and sorcery is mere intuition or deception, there are real supernatural powers and personalities that can work through these practices. She smiled affirmatively.

But then I cautioned her: "Although your spiritual powers might be real, they're definitely not good." I showed her the biblical warnings, such as those from the apostles Paul and John, as well as some of the clear condemnations of occult spiritual practices in the Old Testament.[32] I don't know whether my admonition convinced her or not, but you'd better believe that the rest of the class was paying close attention at that point.

I hope these two guidelines serve you well, at least as first steps in thinking about mystical claims and encounters:

Feel ≠ Real
and
Real ≠ Good

∞

Before we end this chapter, let me assure you of something you might not expect: I genuinely believe that mystical encounters are events we will sometimes *feel*; they can, in fact, be *real*; and they are often *good*—but only when they come from the living God as a way to communicate his love, truth, encouragement, or guidance to us.

I've spent most of this chapter laying out cautions and tests. I needed to do this because so many people are misled by mystical experiences—either imagined or real but dangerous. Let me close now with a few examples of encounters that I trust and celebrate because I believe they pass the various tests and their claims are corroborated by other kinds of evidence.

1. *The apostle Paul, when he was still known as Saul, had an unexpected encounter with God:*

Saul was uttering threats with every breath and was eager to kill the Lord's followers. So he went to the high priest. He requested letters addressed to the synagogues in Damascus, asking for their cooperation in the arrest of any followers of the Way he found there. He wanted to bring them—both men and women—back to Jerusalem in chains.

As he was approaching Damascus on this mission, a light from heaven suddenly shone down around him. He fell to the ground and heard a voice saying to him, "Saul! Saul! Why are you persecuting me?"

"Who are you, lord?" Saul asked.

And the voice replied, "I am Jesus, the one you are persecuting! Now get up and go into the city, and you will be told what you must do."

The men with Saul stood speechless, for they heard the sound of someone's voice but saw no one! Saul picked himself up off the ground, but when he opened his eyes he was blind. So his companions led him by the hand to Damascus. He remained there blind for three days and did not eat or drink....

Ananias went and found Saul. He laid his hands on him and said, "Brother Saul, the Lord Jesus, who appeared to you on the road, has sent me so that you might regain your sight and be filled with the Holy Spirit." Instantly something like scales fell from Saul's eyes, and he regained his sight. Then he got up and was baptized. Afterward he ate some food and regained his strength.[33]

2. *Saint Augustine, before he was in any way saintly, struggled with temptation and with what to do with his life:*

I was overcome with anger with myself, knowing what I needed to do but seemingly not able to do it. I gave way to my tears, and in my misery I cried out to [God] in bitter sorrow.

All at once I heard a young child's voice from a nearby garden singing over and over, "Take it and read, take it and read." I looked up, dried my tears, telling myself that this could only be a divine message intended for me to open the Scripture and read what I should find there. I hurried to find the book of Paul's writings, and there opened to Romans 13:13-14. "Not in reveling and drunkenness, not in lust and wantonness, not in quarrels and rivalries. Rather, arm yourselves with the Lord Jesus Christ; spend no more thought on nature and nature's appetites."

In a moment all the darkness of doubt was dispelled and the light of confidence flooded my soul.[34]

3. *Blaise Pascal, the eminent French mathematician, wrote an in-the-moment account as he powerfully experienced God's presence during what came to be known as "la nuit de feu"—the night of fire:*

From about half past ten in the evening until about half past midnight: *FIRE*.

> The God of Abraham, the God of Isaac, the God of Jacob.
> Not of the philosophers and intellectuals.
> Certitude, certitude, feeling, joy, peace!
> The God of Jesus Christ. My God and your God. . . .
> Forgetfulness of the world and of everything except God. . . .
> The grandeur of the human soul.
> Oh just Father, the world has not known you, but I have
> known you. Joy, joy, joy, tears of joy . . .[35]

Perhaps you, too, have had, or will have, some kind of a mystical encounter. If so, let me encourage you, in the words of the apostle Paul—who spoke out of his own experience, as well as from God's wisdom—not to scoff at it, but to "test everything that is said. Hold on to what is good. Stay away from every kind of evil."[36]

CHAPTER SEVEN

"I'VE GOTTA *SEE IT* TO BELIEVE IT"

Logic, Evidence, and Science

The student Doko came to a Zen master and said, "I am seeking the truth. In what state of mind should I train myself, so as to find it?"

Said the master, "There is no mind, so you cannot put it in any state. There is no truth, so you cannot train yourself for it."

"If there is no mind to train, and no truth to find, why do you have these monks gather before you every day to study Zen and train themselves for this study?"

"But I haven't an inch of room here," said the master, "so how could the monks gather? I have no tongue, so how could I call them together or teach them?"

"Oh, how can you lie like this?" asked Doko.

"But if I have no tongue to talk to others, how can I lie to you?" asked the master.

Then Doko said sadly, "I cannot follow you. I cannot understand you."

"I cannot understand myself," said the master.

∞

A monk came to the master Nansen and asked: "Tell me, is there some teaching that no master has ever taught?"

Nansen said, "There is."

The monk asked, "Can you tell me what it is?"

Nansen said, "It is not Buddha. It is not things. It is not thinking."

∞

Little Toyo was only a twelve-year-old pupil at the Kennin temple, but he wanted to be given a *koan* to ponder, just like the more advanced students. So one evening, at the proper time, he went to the room of Mokurai, the master, struck the gong softly to announce his presence, bowed, and sat before the master in respectful silence.

Finally the master said: "Toyo, show me the sound of two hands clapping."

Toyo clapped his hands.

"Good," said the master. "Now show me the sound of one hand clapping."

Toyo was silent. Finally he bowed and left to consider this problem.

The next night he returned and struck the gong with one palm. "That is not right," said the master. The next night Toyo returned and played geisha music with one hand. "That is not right," said the master. The next night Toyo returned and imitated the dripping of water. "That is not right," said the master. The next night Toyo returned, and imitated the cricket scraping his leg. "That is still not right," said the master.

For ten nights Toyo tried new sounds. At last he stopped coming to the master. For a year he thought of every sound, and discarded them all, until finally he reached enlightenment.

He returned respectfully to the master. Without striking the gong, he sat down and bowed. "I have heard sound without sound," he said.[1]

∞

Does this all make sense to you? If it doesn't—in case you're not yet enlightened into the world of Zen Buddhism and its paradoxical stories called *koans*—here's a Zen "explanation" of that last one:

> Silence is not silence and sound is not sound. In Zen you can find silence in sound and sound in silence. The sound is always there and the silence is always there, they are THE SAME. Get rid of DEFINITIONS of what silence is and what sound is. Drop conventional thinking and listen when you see a hand. That will lead to understanding of Zen which is freedom.[2]

Aren't you glad they cleared that up for us?

Actually, if you're left scratching your head, I think it's a good thing. These little riddles are designed with the goal of making us realize the limitations and the ultimate futility of logical reasoning so we'll give up on analytical thought altogether—which is regarded as a vital step toward real enlightenment.

Many view this as a hallmark of Eastern thinking; logic as we know it is somehow "Western" and doesn't apply to other cultures. The people in those cultures supposedly see beyond our limited and confining realm of logic, as well as the illusory physical world of maya, and operate on a higher, more spiritual plane.

Intriguing as it might sound, this bifurcated, East vs. West understanding of the world has serious problems. These flaws are illustrated by a story about Ravi Zacharias, an author who lives in the United States but was born and raised in India, when he gave a talk at an American university:

> Ravi was assailed by one of the university's professors for not understanding Eastern logic. During the Q & A period the professor charged, "Dr. Zacharias, your presentation about Christ claiming and proving to be the only way to salvation is wrong for people in India because you're using 'either-or' logic. In the East we don't use 'either-or' logic—that's Western. In the East we use 'both-and' logic. So salvation is not *either* through Christ *or* nothing else, but *both* Christ *and* other ways."
>
> Ravi found this very ironic because, after all, he grew up in India. Yet here was a Western-born, American professor telling Ravi that he didn't understand how things really worked in India! This was so intriguing that Ravi accepted the professor's invitation to lunch in order to discuss it further.
>
> One of the professor's colleagues joined them for lunch, and as he and Ravi ate, the professor used every napkin and

placemat on the table to make his point about the two types of logic—one Western and one Eastern.

"There are two types of logic," the professor kept insisting.

"No, you don't mean that," Ravi kept replying.

"I absolutely do!" maintained the professor.

This went on for better than thirty minutes: The professor lecturing, writing, and diagramming. He became so engrossed in making his points that he forgot to eat his meal, which was slowly congealing on his plate.

Upon finishing his own meal, Ravi interrupted. "Professor, I think we can resolve this debate very quickly with just one question."

Looking up from his furious drawing, the professor paused and said, "Okay, go ahead."

Ravi leaned forward, looked directly at the professor, and asked, "Are you saying that when I'm in India, I must use *either* the 'both-and logic' *or* nothing else?"

The professor looked blankly at Ravi, who then repeated his question with emphasis: "Are you saying that when I'm in India, I must use *either*," Ravi paused for effect, "the 'both-and logic' *or*," another pause, "nothing else?" . . .

After glancing sheepishly at his colleague, the professor looked down at his congealed meal and mumbled, "The *either-or* does seem to emerge, doesn't it?" Ravi added, "Yes, even in India we look both ways before we cross the street because it is *either* me *or* the bus, not both of us!"[3]

Logic really is inescapable. Both sides of a contradictory statement cannot be true—on either side of the ocean. The intellectual conundrums of the Zen teacher or Eastern guru may confound some folks with their mix of cleverness and nonsense, but they certainly do not defeat real logic.

In reality, their riddles were logically constructed to appear as if they defeat clear thinking. Why? The claim made, as we saw above, is that this is to help people let go of logic and move toward some kind of esoteric experience called "enlightenment." But what these stories actually seem to do, if anything, is confuse people to the point where they give up on their *own* thinking and accept the *guru's* rationale instead. In the end, logic is not vanquished; it's just a question of *whose* "logic"—and thus whose leadership and influence—will prevail.

In fact, apart from using so-called Western logic, which the Zen *koans* are meant to defeat, nobody would even be able to understand anything about these self-contradictory stories. For example, regardless of what the teacher might want to say about the sound or nonsound supposedly made by the one hand clapping, he is still relying on the mind of his student to logically understand what a *hand* is (and not confuse it with a *walrus* or a *Ping-Pong ball*), what it means to *clap* (versus *parachute* or *hiccup*), and what is being discussed when he uses the word *sound* (rather than *appear, taste, smell, feel,* or *itch*). The very definitions of these words—and even the mental thoughts formed before the words are spoken—depend on the logical mind understanding that you're talking about these specific things and actions rather than any others.

Even the incomprehensible admonition we quoted earlier, telling us to "get rid of definitions," presumes that the one receiving those instructions (as well as the one giving them) understands the correct definition of *definitions*, as well as what is entailed in trying to get rid of something.

What all this means is that, in effect, the Eastern teacher must first borrow from so-called Western logic before trying to undermine it—which, of course, is thoroughly self-defeating. And when it comes to choosing your faith, it's an exceedingly bad idea to base it on any point of view that is self-defeating or that illogically tries to downplay the importance of logic.

∞

Let's take a step back and more broadly examine this sixth, and final, approach to choosing our beliefs—which we'll describe as the *Evidential* faith path. Here, we're actually dealing with two sides of the same coin: logic and experience. This includes the reasoning of the mind (which we've been discussing) combined with real-world information that we gain through the five senses. William Lane Craig eloquently sums up this approach:

> Logic and facts are the keys to showing soundly that a conclusion is true. Since a proposition that is logically contradictory is necessarily false and so cannot be the conclusion of a sound argument, and since a proposition validly inferred from factually true premises ought to be regarded as factually true, one may generalize these notions to say that a world view ought to be regarded as true just in case it is logically consistent and fits all the facts known in our experience. Such a test for truth has been called *systematic consistency*: "consistency" meaning obedience to the laws of logic and "systematic" meaning fitting all the facts known by experience.[4]

For the record, the use of these two elements, logic and fact, could technically have been divided into two distinct approaches. And actually, they were at one time, when the rationalists of Continental Europe—mostly under the influence of René Descartes (of "I think, therefore I am" fame)—competed for philosophical dominance with the British empiricists, the best known of whom was David Hume.

The argument from the rationalist point of view was that the senses can't be trusted, and therefore, real knowledge—of the indisputable kind—was limited to the logical and mathematical. Just consider, these folks would say, the simple phenomenon of a stick appearing to be bent when you put it part way into water. Your eyes tell you it's crooked, but your rational mind knows better. So logic wins over sensory data.

Real knowledge comes when the logical, organizing power of the mind is applied to the real-world experience and data gained through the senses.

The empiricists, on the other hand, would counter that the logical mind neither knows nor proves anything without engaging in the real world. Even the bent-stick problem is solved by either feeling the stick to confirm that it is still straight or by pulling it out of the water and looking at it again to see that it's not crooked. Either way, sensory investigation wins over logical theorizing.

This debate went on for about a century (only philosophers can debate things like this for *that* long). Finally, along came a German thinker named Immanuel Kant, who proposed what would seem to be an obvious solution (as you're reading this with your *eyes* and thinking about it with your *mind*). Kant observed that we need *both*. Real knowledge comes when the logical, organizing power of the mind is applied to the real-world experience and data gained through the senses. These two elements are examples of fundamental, undeniable realities. To even try to argue against them, you must first employ them. And, apart from them, nothing could be known.

∞

How is this Evidential approach applied in real life? The *logical aspect* forms a primarily negative screen by which an argument or teaching is tested. We've been applying this test to many of the religious truth claims throughout this book, including my efforts to show the self-defeating contradictions of Zen Buddhism and Eastern thought. We've also applied the law of non-contradiction to the claims of Islam, whose leaders say that they (1) believe in Jesus and his teachings as a true prophet of God, but (2) deny Jesus' historical claims regarding his identity as the Son of God, his death on the cross, and his resurrection from the dead.

We've also applied the same kind of logic to the Mormon claim that they (1) believe and teach the truths of the Bible but (2) are polytheistic in their teachings (belief in the existence of many gods), which contradicts the consistent monotheistic teachings of the Bible (belief in only one God).

One more example, which we haven't discussed previously, would be the claims of the Baha'i religion when it states that (1) Islam and its teachings are true; (2) Christianity and its teachings are also true (including, apparently, both sides of the contradictory statements from Islam and Christianity about Jesus' identity, death, and resurrection); (3) Judaism is also true, including their hope in a not-yet-seen Messiah (who is also, according to Baha'i teachings, the return of Christ for the Christians, which leaders of Judaism reject); and (4) each of these, and several other religions as well, are all true and all fit under their own doctrines of Bahaism (which at various points contradicts all the religions it claims to unite, which also contradict each other).

Therefore, it seems that the Baha'i faith earns the dubious honor of being the best example of rational incoherence in a religion. So, *let the buyer beware.* Having logical contradictions at the heart of a religion's teachings is not just a problem—it is self-defeating to the entire faith system.

∞

Now let's look at the other side of the coin: *sensory experience.* This aspect—which wields the weapons commonly described as *facts* or *evidence*—can be used to investigate a faith claim and show it to be false (where it touches on facts related to the tangible world, as opposed to the purely mystical). It can also be used to build a positive case, as I'll show in later chapters.

In terms of examining, debunking, or affirming truth claims, experiential tests can be applied through a variety of disciplines. The most obvious is *general science*, known for testing theories and beliefs with physical observation and experimentation. (An example of this that we've discussed in the religious realm has to do with the ethnic origins of Native American people groups— namely, does DNA testing support the claim in the *Book of Mormon* that Native Americans are of Middle Eastern descent, or are they of Asian descent as is more commonly believed?) In our culture, the observation and experimentation approach has become so synonymous with knowledge and education that, for most people, the word *scientific* has come to mean that something is tested, reliable, and therefore almost certainly true. The public's level of trust probably goes beyond what is warranted, especially when we understand that scientific study can only provide moderate to higher levels of probability, not absolute proof. But the trust tends to be there just the same.

When we want to investigate claims related to the past, we look to *history*, which is based on events as they were experienced and recorded by people who were actually there, or later by historians using the most reliable records available to them. Much of our knowledge is based on historical accounts, which can be used to confirm or contradict various religious writings and teachings. (For example: What *did* Jesus really say about his identity and his mission?)

In our culture, the word scientific *has come to mean that something is tested, reliable, and therefore almost certainly true.*

I might add that there has been growing skepticism in our culture about the trustworthiness of historical knowledge. This is especially true after disillusioning revelations have surfaced in recent years, such as the discovery that George Washington apparently did not chop down a cherry tree and then nobly confess, "Father, I cannot tell a lie; I did it with my little hatchet." (If you hadn't heard that this story has been discredited, I'm sorry to be the one to break it to you.) If we can't believe classic stories like this one—which many of us have been taught since childhood—then what historical claims *can* we trust?

Before we disparage the usefulness of history altogether,

remember that it is often the further application of the same discipline that brings the better answer. So, for example, in our earlier discussion of the bent-stick illusion, the very senses that tricked the eyes about the stick in the water were the same senses that, with further investigation, brought better information and straightened out our understanding. Similarly, the craft of history that inadvertently taught us the myth about George Washington is the same craft that brought us further and more accurate information, clearing away the myth from the reality. It was *historians* who helped to straighten out the historical record. What we need is not the denial of historical knowledge, but extra vigilance and care in investigating the facts that undergird the historical record.

∞

Archaeology is another discipline that can give us relevant information about faith-related truth claims. In fact, archaeological research has repeatedly reinforced and confirmed biblical claims from both the Old and New Testaments. The following story about the once-doubted existence of the Hittite nation is one of many examples that could be cited:

> The Hittites played a prominent role in Old Testament history. They interacted with biblical figures as early as Abraham and as late as Solomon. They are mentioned in Genesis 15:20 as people who inhabited the land of Canaan. First Kings 10:29 records that they purchased chariots and horses from King Solomon. The most prominent Hittite is Uriah, the husband of Bathsheba. The Hittites were a powerful force in the Middle East from 1750 B.C. until 1200 B.C. Prior to the late nineteenth

century, nothing was known of the Hittites outside the Bible, and many critics alleged that they were an invention of the biblical authors.

In 1876, a dramatic discovery changed this perception. A British scholar named A. H. Sayce found inscriptions carved on rocks in Turkey. He suspected that they might be evidence of the Hittite nation. Ten years later, more clay tablets were found in Turkey at a place called Boghaz-koy. German cuneiform expert Hugo Winckler investigated the tablets and began his own expedition at the site in 1906.

Winckler's excavations uncovered five temples, a fortified citadel and several massive sculptures. In one storeroom he found over ten thousand clay tablets. One of the documents proved to be a record of a treaty between Rameses II and the Hittite king. Other tablets showed that Boghaz-koy was the capital of the Hittite kingdom. Its original name was Hattusha and the city covered an area of 300 acres. The Hittite nation had been discovered![5]

Our *justice system* is also based on an evidential foundation. When someone is on trial, for example, the ultimate questions that matter are not related to theories, suspicions, or prejudices about the person's appearance, past, or proclivities, but to the facts relevant to the actual accusation that can be "proven beyond a reasonable doubt." These are established through information regarding what any eyewitnesses saw; sounds a reliable person heard; incriminating evidence such as fingerprints, footprints, hair, or blood found in the area; written documents and receipts, bank records, surveillance videos, and so forth. Our society has shown that we have enough confidence in the study of these kinds of sensory and experiential data to draw conclusions that allow us to throw people into prison for life—or sometimes even put them to death—based on what we can learn in this way.

Ordinary observation is also built on the kind of sensory experience we've been discussing. In fact, this is the primary way we learn things day in and day out, sometimes even in the spiritual realm. For example, was that person who claims to be healed really sick or physically impaired in the first place? Does this religious teacher give evidence in his or her life of being a humble, honest, ethical, trustworthy person? Is there any reason to believe this guy riding next to me in my car is really the Holy Spirit?

Just as we rely on the Evidential approach in ordinary, everyday life, it can also be extremely valuable in the realm of our religious understanding.

∞

So, just as we rely on the Evidential approach in ordinary, everyday life, it can also be extremely valuable in the realm of our religious understanding. For some of us, this is the primary path we've used in figuring out our own faith.

But we need to address the way in which some people in our society are applying the information that comes through logic and experience. You see, along the way, some leading thinkers moved from the general use and application of scientific knowledge, to an ideology that determines in advance what kinds of conclusions and beliefs will be deemed acceptable within the intellectual community. In effect, these people hijacked science—which historically had been dominated by people of genuine faith—and transformed it into something else, often referred to as *scientism*, "the belief that the scientific method is the only method for discovering truth."[6]

The broad ideology of scientism is very similar to a once-popular school of thought called *logical positivism*:

> The father of modern scientism was the atheist Auguste Comte, who also began a religion of secular humanism. Comte's view is also known as positivism, an ancestor to the logical positivism of A. J. Ayer.[7]
>
> Logical Positivism is a school of thought that . . . took an anti-metaphysical stand and developed a principle of empirical verification by which all *but* tautologies [logical statements] and empirical statements were considered meaningless. . . . All God-talk was pronounced to be literally nonsense.[8]
>
> [The] decoupling of theology from science and the redefinition of science that underlay it was justified less by argument than by an implicit assumption about the characteristic features of all scientific theories—features that presumably could distinguish theories of a properly scientific (that is, positivistic) bent from those tied to unwelcome metaphysical or theological moorings. . . . Such theories have been declared "unscientific by definition."[9]

To summarize, the doctrine behind scientism, and its narrower expression (logical positivism), is that only naturalistic explanations (as opposed to supernatural ones) will be considered as possible causes or explanations, regardless of the topic or the strength of the evidence presented. In effect, it is an attempt to decide by decree that science will be, from this point forward and forevermore, atheistic. By definition, God and all things spiritual are ruled out in advance from being true or real.

Here's how this plays out on a practical level: Someone may claim to have been miraculously healed—but we know that can't actually happen, so we'll figure out what must have occurred, based on purely natural causes. Or, eyewitnesses may have written down clear and compelling testimonies concerning the miracles of Jesus—especially about his resurrection—but miracles are merely myths and fairy tales, so we'll investigate the real story or psychology behind these obviously fanciful claims.

Consider the approach that atheist Richard Dawkins takes in his book *The Blind Watchmaker*:

> Biology is the study of complicated things that give the appearance of having been designed for a purpose.[10]
>
> Yet the living results of natural selection overwhelmingly impress us with the appearance of design as if by a master watchmaker, impress us with the illusion of design and planning.[11]
>
> Animals give the appearance of having been designed by a theoretically sophisticated and practically ingenious physicist or engineer.[12]
>
> We have seen that living things are too improbable and too beautifully "designed" to have come into existence by chance.[13]

But Dawkins proceeds to write as if it is completely out of the question to even *consider* the idea that these examples of apparent design could really point toward an Intelligent Designer, as they so clearly and powerfully seem to do. Instead, modeling the mind-set of scientism, he substitutes his own theory, which seems much more improbable, something he describes as "the blind watchmaker." This is Dawkins's term for natural selection, which, he tell us, "is the explanation for the existence and apparently purposeful form of all life, [but] has no purpose in mind. It has no mind and no mind's eye. It does not plan for the future. It has no vision, no foresight, no sight at all."[14]

This pattern runs throughout Dawkins's writings. He exhibits what might best be described as a religious faith in his atheistic presuppositions and never gives serious consideration to God, who he claims "*almost* certainly does not exist," as the cause behind anything we observe.[15] It's no wonder that a popular magazine titled its review of Dawkins's latest book as "Hysterical Scientism: The Ecstasy of Richard Dawkins."[16]

How might we address those scientists and others who have bought into scientism, and ruled out God, and persuade them to reconsider their presuppositions and prejudices?

Scientism says, in effect, "We've already ruled out the supernatural portion of the list of possible explanations; now bring us your claims about gods, angels, and elves, and we'll try to help you sort it all out."

But just imagine for a moment that there is a real God who actually created the world; who did miracles through Jesus, including raising him from the dead; and who chooses occasionally to show his love and power by healing people of various sicknesses and ailments. (By the way, if God really exists, these things would be mere child's play for him.) Now, assuming these things are true and supposing we wanted to be God's advocates, how might we address those scientists and others who have bought into scientism, and ruled out God by definition, and persuade them to reconsider their presuppositions and prejudices and see that God is real and truly behind these things?

I don't know the answer, because these folks have already decided to limit their range of possible causes, as if science *must*, for some unknown reason or by some unwritten but absolute law, exclude any possibility of a supernatural cause or causal agent. But how *scientific* is that? Isn't it closed minded to say, "Well, even if theoretically there could be a real intelligence in the universe that I don't understand and can't see, I'm resolutely unwilling to consider the possibility of his being involved in the world"? It's like they're covering their eyes and then complaining that they can't see.

What's interesting to me is that the antitheistic philosophy in which these people are placing their trust does not even live up to its own criteria. When scientism says that the scientific method is the only method for discovering truth, it seems to overlook the fact that scientism itself cannot be proven scientifically. The scientific method is unable to prove that it is the only method for discovering truth, so the philosophy of scientism fails by its own standard.

That probably explains the reasons behind what happened over time to logical positivism, which was historically the most articulate and best known expression of scientism. Roy Abraham Varghese writes:

> As any history of philosophy will show, logical positivism
> did indeed come to grief by the 1950s because of its internal
> inconsistencies. In fact, Sir Alfred Ayer himself . . . stated:
> "Logical positivism died a long time ago. I don't think much of
> *Language, Truth and Logic* [Ayer's earlier book that originally

taught logical positivism] is true. . . . When you get down to
detail, I think it's full of mistakes which I spent the last fifty
years correcting or trying to correct."[17]

There we have it—the primary founder of logical positivism declaring defeat for the school of thought that he had
helped launch, along with a confession that the whole system
was fraught with problems and mistakes. So, where does that
leave the thinking of scientism today? Strangely, we're seeing a
resurgence of militant anti-God, antisupernatural, science-ori-
ented books. Varghese, who is the author of numerous popular
books on the interplay between faith and science, describes this
recent phenomenon:

> The year of the "new atheism" was 2006 (the phrase was first
> used by *Wired* magazine in November 2006). From Daniel
> Dennett's *Breaking the Spell* and Richard Dawkins's *The God
> Delusion* to Lewis Wolpert's *Six Impossible Things Before
> Breakfast*, Victor Stenger's *The Comprehensible Cosmos*,
> and Sam Harris's *The End of Faith* (published in 2004, but the
> sequel to which, *Letter to a Christian Nation*, came out in 2006),
> the exponents of a look-back-in-anger, take-no-prisoners type
> of atheism were out in force. What was significant about these
> books was not their level of argument—which was modest,
> to put it mildly—but the level of visibility they received both
> as bestsellers and as a "new" story discovered by the media.
> The "story" was helped even further by the fact that the authors
> were as voluble and colorful as their books were fiery.
>
> The chief target of these books is, without question,
> organized religion of any kind, time, or place. Paradoxically,
> the books themselves read like fundamentalist sermons. . . .

But how do these works and authors fit into the larger philosophical discussion of God of the last several decades? The answer is they don't.

In the first place, they refuse to engage the real issues involved in the question of God's existence. . . . Second, they show no awareness of the fallacies and muddles that led to the rise and fall of logical positivism. Those who ignore the mistakes of history will have to repeat them at some point. . . .

It would be fair to say that the "new atheism" is nothing less than a regression to the logical positivist philosophy that was renounced by even its most ardent proponents. In fact, the "new atheists," it might be said, do not even rise to logical positivism.[18]

That's a scathing indictment of a seemingly powerful popular movement—one that is trying to hold science hostage to artificially induced anti-God dogmas. But the good news is that we don't have to play along with them. Instead, we can support the growing numbers of philosophers, scientists, and educators who remain open to *all* the possible answers to the biggest and most profound questions of our day, including the existence of God.

We can follow the example of a man who until very recently was recognized as the world's leading philosophical atheist: Antony Flew. Flew said in a recent interview, "My life has been guided by the principle of Plato's Socrates: Follow the evidence, wherever it leads."[19] Relentlessly pursuing the evidence, Flew let go of his atheistic beliefs at age eighty-one, publicly embracing the view that there is a God—an Intelligent Designer—behind the creation of the universe.

Lee Strobel and I had the chance to spend some time with Flew and talk to him about these matters. Lee asked him what specifically had prompted such dramatic changes in his point of view. Flew's response focused on one particular issue: "Einstein felt that there must be intelligence behind the integrated complexity of the physical world. If that is a sound argument, the integrated complexity of the *organic* world is just inordinately greater—all the creatures are complicated pieces of design. So an argument that is important about the physical world is immeasurably stronger when applied to the biological world."[20]

Apparently neither Einstein nor Flew, two of the brightest minds of the past century, had any sense that good science or the Evidential approach was limited to the realm of the natural. Both found its compelling mix of logic and experience to be what it can also be for you and for me: a powerful pathway toward finding a meaningful faith.

CHAPTER EIGHT

"I'M THINKING ABOUT HOW I *THINK*— AND *CHOOSE*"

Assessing the Six Faith Paths

I'VE GOT BETTER QUESTIONS THAN I HAVE ANSWERS
BETTER DREAMS THAN I HAVE PLANS
I'VE GOT BETTER THOUGHTS THAN I HAVE ACTIONS
SO I BUILT MY HOUSE ON WHAT I THOUGHT WAS
    SOLID GROUND
BUT I KNOW IT COULD BE SAND

Todd Agnew, "Prelude"[1]

"How do you know that you know what you know?"

My friend Bob Passantino was famous for asking people questions like that—and then keeping them up until all hours of the night talking about it. He was relentless. *Tenacious* would be a better word to describe him; he was an unyielding philosophical bulldog. He wouldn't let up on his victims—I mean his *friends*—until they reached either clarity or complete exhaustion. Usually, the two came at about the same time.

I didn't mind talking about what I thought. And I didn't mind talking about what I thought about what other people thought. But spending hours thinking about *how* I think and talking about *why* I think those thoughts make sense, as well as trying to explain how I know what I think I know—that was all a pretty big stretch at that time in my life. But like some kind of mental workout routine, it was good for me and my intellectual development, as well as for my spiritual growth.

∞

Up to this point, my goal in this book has been to examine how we know what we think we know and to consider whether we're on the best path toward choosing our faith. After all, there are many leaders, teachers, and friends; books, broadcasts, and blogs; articles, e-mails, and editorials; consultants, counselors, and gurus; professors, preachers, and even podcasts—all kinds of influences that are constantly trying to get us to accept their ideas, claims, and "truths." They want us to choose *their* faith. And they usually want us to adopt their method of choosing, too. But we must learn to critically evaluate their claims, their particular approaches to assessing those claims, and the evidence for and against their teachings. And then we need to make an informed choice of our own.

So let's distill what we've discussed so far and apply it to the realm of spiritual beliefs. In order to do this, we're going to break down the three words in the book's title—*choosing your faith*—and use them as the themes for this chapter and the next two. We'll start with *choosing*.

Choosing Your Faith

I'm convinced there's nothing more important than choosing your faith—intentionally and wisely. But I'm also certain that making a good decision about your faith requires not only facts and information but also careful consideration about how that information will be processed and weighed. We tend to follow one of several *faith paths,* and the particular path we pick—or even passively adopt—can have a great bearing on which beliefs we end up embracing. Because the six paths are so vital to the process of choosing wisely, let's review them and see the impact that each can have on this whole activity of *choosing*.

There's nothing more important than choosing your faith—intentionally and wisely. But making a good decision requires not only facts and information but also careful consideration.

#1: The Relativistic Faith Path

The first approach, which we discussed in chapter 2, flows out of a relativistic viewpoint that says truth is merely a subjective by-product of the mind. In other words, it's something you invent rather than something you discover. So, as long as what's real is produced by what is thought, then why not just pragmatically think and believe things that work for you, serve your needs, and fit with whatever else you've already chosen to believe?

It's not hard to see how this mind-over-matter methodology would lead someone to ignore discomforting information or challenging data and choose instead to focus on ideas that fit the desired outcome. So if *what works* is to think that we are our own god, as New Age thinking tells us, or if *what fits* our beliefs and desires is to decide that morality is merely a by-product of our culture but really not binding on us as individuals, then it's not hard to imagine some of the places this pragmatic thinking can lead us. Why not just do whatever feels right? If we look around us, or simply watch the evening news, we'll see some of the self-serving things people do once they are convinced that all that matters is inventing and living out their own private reality.

This approach can also lead to a not-too-distant cousin of pragmatism and relativism known as *syncretism*—which is the combination of new ideas and old ideas even when all these ideas conflict with one another. Instead of choosing one faith, it's the collecting of a bouquet of spiritual ideas that may seem attractive or useful. This is what one writer described as "iPod Religion,"[2] the goal of which is to create our own personalized playlist of ideas that seem good to us.

A classic example of syncretism is the blending of Catholicism with tribal voodoo practices that is often done in parts of South America. The two really don't mix, but people choose the parts they like from each and put them together anyway.

Syncretism was also reflected in the words of Britain's Prince Charles when he let it be known that upon his becoming king of England—and therefore head of the Anglican Church—he would like to take the title of "Defender of Faith," rather than the traditional "Defender of *the* Faith."[3] After all, why should we limit ourselves to just one religious option when there are so many to choose from?

Closer to home, there was a seventeen-year-old California girl who said, "I mean, I go to church, but I'm not like, 'Oh my god, I have to do what God tells me'—I'm not like that."[4] And actress Goldie Hawn said this in an online interview with Beliefnet: "The interesting part of my spiritual life is studying as much as you can. Islam and Buddhism and Hinduism and Shamanism and Judaism, Christianity—you try to learn what the precepts are, what the religion is, and ultimately, it's based in the same thought, it's based in the same outcome, you know." Then she added in a whisper, "It just has a different façade."[5]

Where do syncretism, relativism, and pragmatism take you? Pretty much anywhere you'd like to go—but you're probably not going to enjoy the actual long-term outcome.

Where do syncretism, relativism, and pragmatism take you? Pretty much anywhere you'd like to go—at least in your own mind—but you're probably not going to enjoy the actual long-term outcome. It's like the person who gets bad reports back from the lab but chooses not to believe in the unpleasantries of cancer and therefore forgoes treatment. It's far better to look for, discover, and then deal with the real truth—*what is*—and choose a faith that is built on facts and truly faces reality.

My encouragement to you is to abandon imagined beliefs in multiple truths—beliefs that don't work in the everyday world of visible things and therefore don't make sense or provide any truly helpful insights in the invisible world of the spiritual, either. Instead, search for real truth, and when you find it, grab onto it with both hands, and don't let it go.

Although *what works* is not always true, *what's true* usually ends up working out for the best.

#2: The Traditional Faith Path

The second approach, which we examined in chapter 3, is generally passive, relying on hand-me-down beliefs, habits, or traditions that are only as good as the quality of the thinking that got them started in the first place. They may be right, if you're lucky, but they could be wrong. You'll never know until you back up and look into the thinking and evidence behind the traditional beliefs you were raised with to see which, if any, are actually valid and therefore worth holding on to.

One thing's for sure: Because different faith traditions often contradict each other, they can't all be correct. It's important, therefore, to stop and look at them more deeply and cautiously. Examining your faith traditions may actually feel inappropriate and even disrespectful at first, given possible family and cultural expectations that you'll just faithfully "carry on the traditions." But the hero of the story is never the one who simply goes along with the crowd or passively perpetuates the practices of yesteryear. (As my son Matthew likes to quip, "Nostalgia's not what it used to be.") Rather, the person we admire is the man or woman who has the courage to see things anew, if need be—who embraces what's right and then acts on it.

#3: The Authoritarian Faith Path

This third approach, reviewed in chapter 4, is similar to the second one because it's passive, but the beliefs you are handed by an authority figure or organization are often imposed with greater forcefulness and a stronger expectation that you will uncritically receive them. This message can come across in subtle ways, or it can be accompanied by overt threats of relational, financial, or even physical repercussions should you choose not to fit in. Consequently, it sometimes takes even more courage to examine the qualifications of these authorities in our lives along with the ideas that flow from them.

There's no need to announce that you're reconsidering what you've been taught. Instead, just quietly, humbly, and prayerfully examine the evidence that is supposed to support the beliefs you've been handed.

But examine them we must. Authorities, like traditions, often contradict each other in what they teach; therefore, they can't all be correct. And though we all end up living under various authorities, in the spiritual realm we need to test the credentials of those leaders who hold (or who would like to hold) sway over us and our faith, to ensure that they are truly worth following.

If you're currently under a spiritual authority that does your choosing for you, let me encourage you to step back and think for yourself. You really do have the option of whether to let that person or organization keep leading you. But be wise in how you do this. Usually, there's no need to announce that you're reconsidering what you've been taught. Instead, just quietly, humbly, and prayerfully begin to examine the evidence that is supposed to support the beliefs you've been handed. Your research might end up confirming the validity of what you've been taught and actually reinforce the credentials of the leadership you've been under. But it's also possible that you'll find information that leads you to better conclusions and a wiser choice of faith.

Don't settle for simple answers or cave into authoritarian pressures to simply conform. Jesus, himself an authority with impeccable credentials, said, "Keep on asking, and you will receive what you ask for. Keep on seeking, and you will find. Keep on knocking, and the door will be opened to you."[6] He also made a promise to those who would ask and seek consistently and earnestly follow what they learned: "You will know the truth, and the truth will set you free."[7]

#4: The Intuitive Faith Path

The fourth approach, which we looked at in chapter 5, can be helpful at least as a warning light indicating that further investigation is needed. Hunches and instincts, as well as the moral sensibilities available from your inbred conscience, can all build toward a kind of spiritually informed street sense that gives you an idea of what and whom you can trust.

But let me caution you not to consider or choose in a vacuum, apart from more objective criteria. Think of a literal warning light in a busy intersection. The flashing yellow bulb doesn't tell you anything clearly or conclusively. It merely says, "Driver beware." It prompts you to look into matters more deeply by slowing down, heightening your awareness, and scanning the road left and right, searching for more information and data that will help you know how to proceed.

That's a pretty good description of the Intuitive approach when it's working right. It alerts you to danger and prompts you to do whatever it takes to educate your mind and further inform your intuition. In other words, it tells you to investigate more deeply and probably to apply the criteria of other faith paths, especially the sixth path, to confirm and clarify the warnings you've been receiving.

So, heed the yellow light, and look into the reasons behind what you might be sensing. Examine the supporting evidence, especially for whatever you might end up choosing to believe. Let your "gut feelings" confirm what you find, but don't let them lead you into blindly guessing or stumbling around in the dark, hoping to be lucky enough to trip over truth. Rather, turn on the lights through finding and considering additional, clearer information.

#5: The Mystical Faith Path

The fifth approach, explored in chapter 6, is a challenging one to assess. It can be so important and powerful because God sometimes uses direct and perhaps unusual ways to communicate his message to us. But it may also be misleading, if we mistake mere feelings for spiritual realities or misidentify real but dangerous spiritual entities as being good ones that are from God, when they may not be. We need discernment, as well as the willingness to stop and examine what we have experienced, or think we have experienced. The popular slogan in our culture to "question everything" is actually not far off the mark here. The apostle Paul, who had to examine his own mystical experiences at points along his journey, advises us to "test everything that is said. Hold on to what is good."[8]

"Testing everything" flows from both common sense and biblical instruction. It involves comparing what you're experiencing to what you already know to be true—from facts about the world and scriptures that have already passed the test as having real credentials of truth. It's from a passage in one of those proven scriptures that we are given this warning:

> Dear friends, do not believe everyone who claims to speak by the Spirit. You must test them to see if the spirit they have comes from God. For there are many false prophets in the world.[9]

That said, if you have a spiritual experience in which God somehow communicates his love or guidance to you—one that passes the tests and proves to be scripturally sound and trustworthy—then you have a great gift that can powerfully lead you in your life and faith.

#6: The Evidential Faith Path

This final approach, reviewed in chapter 7, was saved until last for a reason. That's because it's the one path that tests—and ultimately supports or undermines—all the others. Its two key elements, *logic* and *sensory experience*, are God-given tools we must use to gain the vast majority of our information, to test truth claims, and ultimately to decide what to believe.[10]

Now, I can imagine some religious folks insisting that I've got it all wrong. They might say that God's revelations, or scriptures, have to set the standard and test the other approaches. I partially agree with this. Writings that claim to be revelations from God, or scripture, once they have "passed the test" themselves and have proven they have the credentials to be established as a trustworthy authority, can and should become a further test of other claims. But even then we must apply logic to make the comparisons.

But if we don't first test whatever is claiming to be scripture, how will we know which so-called scriptures to trust? Certainly there are a number of books and writings out there vying for that authoritative position, and they can't all be right. Unless we want to pick one out arbitrarily, like, for example, the Hindu *Bhagavad Gita*, or the LDS *Book of Mormon*, we're going to have to test the various contenders to figure out which, if any, we can actually trust.

Logic *and* sensory experience *are God-given tools we must use to test truth claims, and ultimately to decide what to believe.*

Again, the instruments to use for that test begin with logic and sensory experience, including the experiences of others from the past that are preserved in reliable historical records. As we've seen, logic and experience are inescapable tools—you can't deny them without using them—so we might as well accept them and learn to use them well. And, as we discussed in chapter 7, these are vehicles that can lead us to truth not only in the physical realm but in the spiritual realm as well. We just need to stay open as we carefully (and prayerfully) follow the evidence wherever it leads.

∞

The Evidential approach tells us logically and empirically that there is one set of truths—based on actual, *what is* reality—that we need to discover and let inform our choice of faiths. We can use these tools to test traditional teachings, religious authorities, intuitive instincts and hunches, and mystical encounters, so we can know which ones are worth believing and holding on to.

Next, let's do the important work of looking more deeply at how the Evidential method, combined with tested and proven elements of the other approaches, can be applied in the real world to lead us to a trustworthy faith. This will be the focus of the next three chapters.

It was also the focus of my friend Bob Passantino, whom I mentioned at the beginning of this chapter. When Bob was young, he was a serious spiritual skeptic who loved to corner Christians and intimidate them with challenging questions. But one day he tried to pick on the wrong person, a seminary student named Gene Kirby. Gene invited him to come to his home—if he was really serious about getting answers—to discuss the issues. Bob took him up on the offer—not just once, but every Tuesday night for about six months. Bob threw every objection he could think of at Gene, who patiently but persistently gave him good answers. Gradually, Bob began to see that there is solid logic and evidence for the Christian faith.

Bob wasn't ready, however, to respond to what he was starting to understand. He frankly didn't like the ramifications it would have on his current lifestyle. Instead, he broke off contact with Gene, joined the National Guard, and left the area for nearly a year. Along the way, he also dabbled in drugs, various philosophies, the martial arts, and Buddhism.

Then, one day, he had a mystical encounter that rocked his world. He was sitting in his Volkswagen Beetle with a friend named Bruce, discussing their concerns about catastrophic things that could happen to the world and what they could do to be ready. Suddenly, Bob "felt the unmistakable and real presence of the Holy Spirit fill the car. Without sound or words, he clearly heard Jesus speaking to him, saying, "None of that matters. You are putting your trust in yourselves instead of in Me. All that matters is that I love you. Follow me. . . . Follow me. . . . Follow me."[11]

Bob turned to Bruce, hesitating as he tried to figure out how to tell him what he was experiencing. "Bruce, none of this matters," Bob ventured. "Jesus is real." Much to Bob's surprise, Bruce responded by bursting out, "Don't you feel the Holy Spirit? We have to follow Jesus! He's calling us!" The two of them sat in the car, enjoying what they were confident was God's presence, until they finally needed to leave.

Bob didn't follow the Mystical path blindly. He knew his subjective experience needed to be tested. He checked it out carefully, including the implications that this encounter might have on his broader beliefs and life.

If you had asked Bob which faith paths helped him on his journey, he would have told you it was a blend of the *Evidential* path (with its mix of logic and real-world data and information) with a touch of tested *mysticism*—which made for a powerful and compelling combination.

He didn't follow the Mystical path blindly. He knew his subjective experience needed to be tested. He checked it out carefully.

When he reached a point of real confidence, he committed himself to what he had discovered through his divine encounter and his spiritual pursuit. He immediately started telling his friends what he had learned and experienced. He answered their questions and challenges (most of which they had originally learned from him) with the answers he had found.

Then he spent the rest of his life helping others in that same search for knowledge and truth. He knew the difference it had made in his own life, and he passionately wanted others to experience what *he* had experienced. Perhaps that's why he was so doggedly persistent.

When Bob died suddenly of heart failure in 2003, his wife, their three children, and their many friends were all in shock. Here's part of what I wrote during the first days after Bob's death, to honor and remember him:

> I'm still reeling over the loss of my wonderful friend and mentor of the last twenty-five years, Bob Passantino. I'll miss his wisdom, his encouragement, his partnership, and especially his humor. There's no one else quite like him. . . .
>
> It was never a good idea to get on the other side of an argument from Bob—he was RIGHT!
>
> You proved it, Bob, through your logic, through your love, and through your life. I, and many others, will be indebted to you throughout eternity.[12]

It was under Bob's influence, and that of a few other key individuals, that I decided to invest my life in helping others find the pathway toward truth—and toward the One who is really true. It's in that spirit that I offer this discussion about ways of choosing, as well as the reasons *to* choose, which I'll present next.

CHAPTER NINE

"HOW CAN I *FIGURE OUT* WHAT TO BELIEVE?"

Part 1: Considering the Logical and Scientific Criteria

At night when all the world's asleep
The questions run so deep
For such a simple man
Won't you please, please tell me what we've
  learned
I know it sounds absurd
But please tell me who I am

Supertramp, "The Logical Song"[1]

I've talked about how I enjoy the outdoors, but I haven't mentioned how I used to take it to the *extreme*. Some of my renegade buddies and I would often get together on weekends to go camping. *In the winter*.

Usually, we'd leave on a Friday afternoon after school. We'd pack our tents, sleeping bags, cooking equipment, flashlights, and our warmest parkas, gloves, scarves, and caps—we'd bring shovels, too. They were used to dig through the snowbanks to get down to the frozen ground where we'd pitch our tents. After getting our tents in place, we'd dig another clearing nearby to build a campfire. The fire wasn't just to cook our food or to tell stories around at night; it was to help us survive the freezing temperatures, which at times dipped below zero.

You might imagine that after setting everything up we'd hurry to cook and eat our dinner, then huddle next to a blazing fire in order to stay warm. Instead, we'd usually stake out the surrounding territory and play capture the flag. You can imagine—a gang of half-crazed guys crawling through the snow and hiding behind stumps and brittle frozen brush in order to capture all the members of the opposing team and win the prize.

After dark, we'd usually go for a moonlit night hike. To this day, it's hard to fully understand why we did this, but sometimes we'd trek for miles, walking for hours through the frigid woods as we joked and laughed, told each other tales, and enjoyed the adventure of it all.

Sometimes we'd get lost.

I'm using the word *lost* loosely. We weren't totally clueless about where we were, but we weren't completely sure, either. This was part of the grand escapade, as we taunted fate and then tried to find our path back to the warmth and safety of our campfire and tents. (I'm just reporting the facts—not recommending weekend activities for you or your kids!)

∞

Applying these experiences to the themes of this book, let me tell you about those moments when we were trying to figure out how to get back to the camp. As our snow-packed jeans began to freeze to our legs, and as our fingers and toes began to go numb, our choices for getting home tended to become quite clear.

First Path: One thing nobody ever did in those moments was say, "My truth is we're already there." That Relativistic approach never even entered our minds. We didn't have the luxury in those moments of trying to rejigger the meaning of truth. All we wanted was the pure *what is* reality of some dry clothes and a warm campfire.

Second Path: If anyone reverted to a Traditional formula, such as "If in doubt, wait it out—they'll come and rescue us," they would quickly be overruled by the others. Clichés didn't cut it when we knew that frostbite would set in before anyone even figured out that they needed to start looking for

Clichés didn't cut it when we knew that frostbite would set in before anyone even figured out to start looking for us.

us. Besides, the way we kept warm was by staying in motion. Traditional solutions *can* provide wisdom, but they must prove themselves to be sensible and trustworthy.

Third Path: If someone tried to play the Authoritarian role, telling us confidently to follow him because he knew the way back to camp, there would be a mixed reaction. On the one hand, we'd pay attention and consider what he said; but on the other hand, we'd want to know how he was so sure of what he claimed to know. Authority wouldn't have worked for us without evidence that the "authority" really knew the landscape (or was in possession of a really good map) and was genuinely confident of the way back to safety.

Fourth Path: What about hunches and intuition? Our first response might be to say, "Forget it." People freeze to death thinking they sense the right way to go, only to wander off into the wilderness. But to be fair, if someone felt strongly about an instinct to go a certain direction, that would at least warrant our consideration—though we would test the hunch by searching for other clues, beyond mere instincts.

Fifth Path: I don't remember anyone ever claiming that they knew the direction back because God had told them. But when you're getting really cold and praying for help, you don't want to rule out the possibility of divine guidance. Still, you'd keep your eyes open and look for clues and confirmation before proceeding too far or too fast.

Sixth Path: The one thing we did consistently that always seemed to work—as evidenced by the fact that I'm here today to write about it—was to apply *logic* and *evidence* to the task of looking for the way back to camp:

> *"That can't be the trail—it crosses to the other side of the riverbed, and we never went across that."*

> *"Just look up. See how the Big Dipper points to the North Star? We've been heading almost due north the whole time, and now we need to reverse our direction and head south."*

"Keep an eye on the horizon. In the moonlight you can make out that high point, with the clump of tall trees near the top—our camp is more-or-less over there."

"This won't be hard: We'll just head west until we get to the old cattle road, and then we'll follow it back all the way to the bridge near our camp."

I think this real-life scenario provides a pretty good picture of the situation we all face as we seek to sort out our own spiritual pathways. And I believe our safety, and ultimately our future, depends on our choosing reliable approaches and applying the right criteria.

Choosing Your Faith

In this section, which will span this chapter and the next two, I'll suggest how you might choose *your* faith by discussing some of the evidence and reasons that have helped me choose *my* faith. I'll offer twenty reasons and examples of evidence that I've found convincing. Though every idea won't be equally compelling to every person, I believe that together they provide a cumulative case that points powerfully toward the unique claims of the Christian worldview.

If you come from a Christian background, I hope these thoughts will strengthen your faith—not just because of tradition or authority but because they hold up factually and logically. If you come from a non-Christian background, I hope you'll carefully consider and weigh these points of evidence, asking for God's guidance as you do. Don't forget the skeptic's prayer—"I do believe, but help me overcome my unbelief!"—even if all you can honestly say is the "help my unbelief" part. (Also, be sure to read chapter 12 where we'll discuss the kinds of barriers that can trip us up on our spiritual journeys.)

I'll describe each argument that follows as an *arrow*—because each one points in a certain direction (as we'll see on the diagram in chapter 12). In this chapter, I'll describe reasons from the realms of logic and science. In the next two chapters, we'll focus on the textual, historical, and experiential areas.

Arrow 1 ⋯⋗ Design in the universe points to an *Intelligent Designer.*

This "argument from design" is based on a mix of observation, intuition, logic, and perhaps a dose of common sense. The classic rendition of this view comes from William Paley in his book *Natural Theology,* published in 1802. Paley's famous argument states that if you find a watch on the ground, you immediately surmise it is not a fluke of nature. Watches, by virtue of their complexity and design, require a watchmaker. Whenever something shows evidence of having been made for a purpose, it points us back instinctively to a cause behind it, or an intelligent designer.

I hope these thoughts will strengthen your faith—not just because of tradition or authority but because they hold up factually and logically.

It really is true. Nobody picks up a watch on the beach and says, "Praise the cosmos! Just look at the wonderful creation the forces of chance have tossed together." But as my friend Cliffe Knechtle says, "If you think the *watch* needs a designer, just glance from the watch to your *hand.* It is far more complex, has far more moving parts, displays much more intricate design, and therefore demands a designer that much more."

This observation is substantiated by this fascinating information from Michael Denton, an Australian molecular biologist, when he talks about a unit of life far smaller than the human hand:

> Perhaps in no other area of modern biology is the challenge posed by the extreme complexity and ingenuity of biological adaptations more apparent than in the fascinating new molecular world of the cell. . . . To grasp the reality of life as it has been revealed by molecular biology, we must magnify a cell a thousand million times until it is twenty kilometers in diameter and resembles a giant airship large enough to cover a great city like London or New York. What we would then see would be an object of unparalleled complexity and adaptive design. On the surface of the cell we would see millions of openings, like the port holes of a vast space ship, opening and closing to allow a continual stream of materials to flow in and out. If we were to enter one of these openings we would find ourselves in a world of supreme technology and bewildering complexity. . . .
>
> Is it really credible that random processes could have constructed a reality, the smallest element of which— a functional protein or gene—is complex beyond our own creative capacities, a reality which is the very antithesis of chance, which excels in every sense anything produced by the intelligence of man?[2]

As breathtaking as that example is, I don't know which is more astounding: the design evident when looking down through a microscope or up through a telescope. The realization that the beauty, order, and grandeur of the universe points us to the divine designer goes back at least as far as King David, the writer of many of the Psalms, when he said some three millennia ago: "The heavens proclaim the glory of God. The skies display his craftsmanship."[3] Hundreds of years later, the apostle Paul picked up on David's theme and added a challenge: "Ever since the world was created, people have seen the earth and sky. Through everything God made, they can clearly see his invisible qualities—his eternal power and divine nature. So they have no excuse for not knowing God."[4]

Before moving on, it's worth mentioning an objection that has been raised by atheists as far back as David Hume and as recently as Richard Dawkins: "The designer hypothesis immediately raises the larger problem of who designed the designer."[5] In other words, at best, design in the universe only points to a finite designer—not an infinite deity.

Three thoughts in response:

1. Even if the existence of a finite designer was all we could deduce from this evidence (which I don't think is the case), this designer must be *incredibly intelligent, amazingly powerful*, and *wonderfully wise* to have invented, designed, and somehow produced all of what we see in the universe, including its 10,000 galaxies and 70 sextillion stars (that's 70,000,000,000,000,000,000,000 —and those are just the ones we can see).[6] Any being of that creative magnitude certainly ought to get our attention, capture our imagination, and would undoubtedly be worth listening to and learning from.

2. We shouldn't stop with the existence of a finite designer,

if that's all we can deduce at first. If the original fact of design in the universe compels us to acknowledge a very wise, very old, and very powerful designer, then that same logic, when applied to the designer himself, should take us at least one step further, right?

In other words, if this amazing, but finite, designer shows such incredible marks of design himself, then who designed and made him? That designer-behind-the-designer must be even more utterly mind-boggling. And if *that* designer is limited in any way, we can only imagine (seriously, we *can't even* imagine) what the being who made *him* must be like. If we fol-

> *Even if the existence of a finite designer was all we could deduce from this evidence, this designer must be* incredibly intelligent, amazingly powerful, *and* wonderfully wise.

low this track back far enough, it seems we're soon approaching an eternal, omniscient, omnipotent, omnipresent God. Indeed, the argument from design will eventually draw us back to an *infinite* designer, who will probably be uncannily similar to the God of Abraham, Isaac, and Jacob described in the Bible.

3. What if this intelligent designer actually went to the effort of revealing what he's like in other ways, beyond just the clues we see in nature? What if he spoke through chosen people, explaining that he's not only an intelligent designer but also an eternal, all-powerful being who cares about his creatures and wants to relate to us?

If he's big enough, strong enough, and smart enough to make this universe, then ought we not at least sit up and take notice regarding whatever else he might want to say to us? The evidence of design leads us to at least consider potential information from revelation.

Arrow 2 ····⟩ Fine tuning in the universe points to an intentional *Fine Tuner*.

The design argument has been a strong one for at least three thousand years. Its logic and intuitive force are hard to escape. But in recent years, scientific discovery has *turbocharged* it. That's because our growing understanding of numerous *constants* in physics points to the fine-tuning of the universe that would enable it to support life.

In his book *The Creator and the Cosmos*, astrophysicist Hugh Ross lists more than two dozen examples of areas in which the universe had to fall within extremely narrow tolerances for any kind of life to exist.[7] The chances of this all happening randomly, he explains, are vanishingly small.

Robin Collins, author of a chapter on fine-tuning in *God and Design: The Teleological Argument and Modern Science*, described the situation in an interview with Lee Strobel:

> When scientists talk about the fine-tuning of the universe, they're generally referring to the extraordinary balancing of the fundamental laws and parameters of physics and the initial conditions of the universe. Our minds can't comprehend the precision of some of them. The result is a universe that has just the right conditions to sustain life. The coincidences are simply too amazing to have been the result of happenstance—as [theoretical physicist, cosmologist, and astrobiologist] Paul Davies said, "the impression of design is overwhelming."

I like to use the analogy of astronauts landing on Mars and finding an enclosed biosphere, sort of like the domed structure that was built in Arizona a few years ago. At the control panel, they find that all the dials for its environment are set just right for life. The oxygen ratio is perfect; the temperature is seventy degrees; the humidity is fifty percent; there's a system for replenishing the air; there are systems for producing food, generating energy, and disposing of wastes. Each dial has a huge range of possible settings, and you can see if you were to adjust one or more of them just a little bit, the environment would go out of whack and life would be impossible. What conclusion would you draw from that? . . .

Some intelligent being had intentionally and carefully designed and prepared it to support living creatures. And that's an analogy for our universe.

Over the past thirty years or so, scientists have discovered that just about everything about the basic structure of the universe is balanced on a razor's edge for life to exist. The coincidences are far too fantastic to attribute this to mere chance or to claim that it needs no explanation. The dials are set too precisely to have been a random accident. Somebody, as [astrophysicist and cosmologist] Fred Hoyle quipped, has been monkeying with the physics.[8]

Strobel and Collins went on to talk about a number of amazing examples of the physics having been "monkeyed with." Here's just one of the mind-stretching points they discussed, called the cosmological constant, which is the energy density of empty space:

"Well, there's no way we can really comprehend it," Collins said. "The fine-tuning has conservatively been estimated to be at least one part in a hundred million billion billion billion billion billion. That would be a ten followed by fifty-three zeroes. That's inconceivably precise. Let's say you were way out in space and were going to throw a dart at random toward Earth. It would be like successfully hitting a bull's eye that's one trillionth of a trillionth of an inch in diameter. That's less than the size of one solitary atom."[9]

If the odds are that small for just this one area to be so precisely tuned to support life, imagine how small the odds become when you factor in another thirty or so. The chances become so small that, as Lee Strobel likes to say, "by comparison, they make the lottery look like a sure bet."

Former atheist Patrick Glynn, in his book *God: The Evidence*, sums it up like this: "As recently as twenty-five years ago, a reasonable person weighing the purely scientific evidence on the issue would likely have come down on the side of skepticism. That is no longer the case. Today, the concrete data point strongly in the direction of the God hypothesis. It is the simplest and most obvious solution."[10]

We have that knowledge today, and it's another powerful pointer to the existence of an amazingly wise God who is behind it all.

William Paley would have salivated back in 1802 to have this astounding scientific support for his contention that watches require a watchmaker. He simply had no way of knowing how amazing the "watch" of this world really is. But we have that knowledge today, and it's another powerful pointer to the existence of an amazingly wise God who is behind it all—one who must care a lot for his creatures, given that he so painstakingly created a suitable habitat for them.

Arrow 3 ····⟩ Information encoded into DNA points to a *Divine Encoder.*

Another compelling example of design comes from the world of biology, specifically the incredible complexity of the information encoded within DNA. Francis Collins, head of the international Human Genome Project that mapped the entire DNA sequence of the human species, describes it like this:

> This newly revealed text was 3 billion letters long, and written in a strange and cryptographic four-letter code. Such is the amazing complexity of the information carried within each cell of the human body, that a live reading of that code at a rate of three letters per second would take thirty-one years, even if reading continued day and night. Printing these letters out in regular font size on normal bond paper and binding them all together would result in a tower the height of the Washington Monument. For the first time on that summer morning this amazing script, carrying within it all of the instructions for building a human being, was available to the world.[11]

The name of Collins's book says it all—*The Language of God*—a title that echoes the words of President Bill Clinton when he stood next to Francis Collins and announced that the amazing genome project had been completed: "We are learning the language in which God created life."[12]

Why all the theological language at a press conference for a scientific breakthrough? Because this was not just an amazing human accomplishment; it unveiled the incredible scope of the real biological language in which information—literally, the library of instructions by which living organisms are put together—is contained and conveyed.

Information is not recorded and communicated by mere chance. Lee Strobel illustrates this truth by contrasting two separate patterns on a beach: one being the ripples in the sand formed by the waves, and the other, the words *John loves Mary*, written in the sand. The wave-drawn patterns may be interesting and even beautiful to look at, but they're randomly formed by nature. The words *John loves Mary*, however, would never be mistaken for something random. Clearly they are a message intended to communicate an idea—one to which John hopes Mary will be receptive.

But if something as simple as "John loves Mary" is obviously intelligent communication, how much more so is the life-giving "message" of DNA, which is, as Francis Collins puts it, "3 billion letters long . . . written in a four-letter code . . . [that is] our own instruction book, previously known only to God"?[13]

So powerful is this evidence that Dean Kenyon, a biophysicist from San Francisco State University who had coauthored a book trying to explain the emergence of life apart from any supernatural involvement, later made a dramatic turnabout. "Kenyon . . . repudiated the conclusions of his own book, declaring that he had come to the point where he was critical of all naturalistic theories of origins. Due to the immense molecular complexity of the cell and the information-bearing properties of DNA, Kenyon now believed that the best evidence pointed toward a designer of life."[14]

Kenyon sums up his own conclusions when he writes, "This

new realm of molecular genetics [is] where we see the most compelling evidence of design on the Earth."[15] Kenyon's words echo the opinion of many other leading scientists and thinkers around the world—and I hope an opinion that you're beginning to adopt as your own: The information encoded in DNA points powerfully to a *Divine Encoder*.

Arrow 4 ┅⟩ The beginning of the universe points to a *Divine Originator*.

The logic is powerful in its simplicity. Consider three statements that make up what is commonly referred to as the cosmological argument:

> Whatever has a beginning has a cause.
>
> The universe had a beginning.
>
> Therefore, the universe had a cause.[16]

Looking at the first statement, it seems obvious that *whatever has a beginning has a cause*. Few people would argue with this. Albert Einstein declared, "The scientist is possessed by a sense of universal causation."[17] The whole methodology of science involves studying effects in order to discover the cause behind them. In fact, this causal connectedness is another one of those inescapable realities. Don't ask me why I say this—because if you do you'll only be making my point. (You'll be trying to get at the cause behind the effect of my statement, which says effects demand causes.)

My friend Chad Meister illustrates this first statement in a real-life scenario: "If I go to the doctor to find out why a lump has begun growing in my throat, I'm not going to be satisfied with his telling me that there's no cause for that lump—that it just sprang up for no reason, with no real cause. Instead, I'm going to go find a new doctor."

If you're a parent, and you go into one of your kids' rooms and find a hole punched in the wall, you're not going to accept a causeless, self-existent hole-in-the-wall theory. Instead, you want a real explanation from your son or daughter—the old-fashioned kind that actually *explains*.

If you loan someone your car, and he brings it back with a fresh dent in the bumper, you don't want to enter into a philosophical discussion about whether or not "dents that begin to exist need a cause"; you just want to know what your friend ran into (and how he's going to pay for the repairs).

If the appearance of lumps, holes, and dents needs a cause, how much more so the original appearance of the universe?

If the appearance of lumps, holes, and dents needs a cause, how much more so the original appearance of the universe?

The second statement in the argument claims that the universe had a beginning. The only option is to say that it is eternal and has simply always been there—an answer akin to the causeless, self-existent hole-in-the-wall theory—or to claim that it popped into existence out of nothing and from nothing: *poof.* But as scholar Norman Geisler winsomely makes clear by quoting the lyrics of a song from *The Sound of Music*, "Nothing comes from nothing, nothing ever could." We really do know better.[18]

So we know the universe had a beginning through commonsense logic—but we know it through modern science, as well. Robert Jastrow, an astronomer and the founding director of NASA's Goddard Institute for Space Studies, summarized the conclusion of decades of scientific research in his groundbreaking book *God and the Astronomers*:

> Five independent lines of evidence—the motions of the galaxies, the discovery of the primordial fireball, the laws of thermodynamics, the abundance of helium in the Universe and the life story of the starts—point to one conclusion; all indicate that the Universe had a beginning.[19]

Jastrow also explains the theory of that amazing beginning, usually referred to in scientific circles as the Big Bang:

> The matter of the Universe is packed together into one dense mass under enormous pressure, and with temperatures ranging up to trillions of degrees. The dazzling brilliance of the radiation in this dense, hot Universe must have been beyond description. The picture suggests the explosion of a cosmic hydrogen bomb. The instant in which the cosmic bomb exploded marked the birth of the Universe.
>
> The seeds of everything that has happened in the Universe since were planted in that first instant; every star, every planet and every living creature in the Universe owes its physical origins to events that were set in motion in the moment of the cosmic explosion. In a purely physical sense, it was the moment of creation.[20]

Stephen Hawking, the popular theoretical physicist, adds perspective on how widespread this understanding is in scientific circles: "Almost everyone now believes that the universe, and time itself, had a beginning at the big bang."[21]

So, both logic and science tell us that the universe had a beginning. And we established earlier that whatever has a beginning has a cause. So the natural conclusion is that *the universe had a cause.*

But that leaves us with the realization that something *outside of the universe* caused it. That "something" would have to be big enough, smart enough, powerful enough, and old enough—not to mention have enough of a creative, artistic flair—to be able to pull off such a grand "effect." That sounds suspiciously similar to the divine being described in the book of Genesis, which starts with these words: "In the beginning God created the heavens and the earth."[22]

Or, as Robert Jastrow puts it famously at the end of *God and the Astronomers,* "For the scientist who has lived by his faith in the power of reason, the story ends like a bad dream. He has scaled the mountains of ignorance; he is about to conquer the highest peak; as he pulls himself over the final rock, he is greeted by a band of theologians who have been sitting there for centuries."[23]

For us, however, the dream can end well: science and scripture converge, pointing in the same direction—toward a divine *Originator*—as together they assist us in wisely choosing our faith.

Arrow 5 ···⟩ The sense of morality throughout the human race points to a *Moral Lawgiver.*

Each of us has an internal standard of morality—but one that is above us and comes from outside of us. Why do I say that the source of this morality is above and outside us? Because everybody has it, but nobody consistently lives up to it. Why would we each invent a code of ethics that we could never quite fulfill, and then employ it to frustrate and condemn ourselves all life long?

I'm not saying that our standards are exactly the same, just that there is a universal sense of right and wrong that every person possesses. We can't get rid of it, short of becoming so jaded that we lose our very humanity (and become *inhumane*). If morality were mere choice or preference, we could much more easily detach ourselves from it.

In the opening section of his classic *Mere Christianity*, titled "Right and Wrong as a Clue to the Meaning of the Universe," C. S. Lewis comments on this sense of morality, which he calls the Law of Nature:

Science and scripture converge, pointing in the same direction— toward a divine Originator—as together they assist us in wisely choosing our faith.

Whenever you find a man who says he does not believe in a real Right and Wrong, you will find the same man going back on this a moment later. He may break his promise to you, but if you try breaking one to him he will be complaining "It's not fair" before you can say Jack Robinson. A nation may say treaties don't matter; but then, next minute, they spoil their case by saying that the particular treaty they want to break was an unfair one. But if treaties do not matter, and if there is no such thing as Right and Wrong—in other words, if there is no Law of Nature—what is the difference between a fair treaty and an unfair one? Have they not let the cat out of the bag and shown that, whatever they say, they really know the Law of Nature just like anyone else?

> It seems, then, we are forced to believe in a real Right
> and Wrong. People may be sometimes mistaken about them,
> just as people sometimes get their sums wrong; but they are
> not a matter of mere taste and opinion any more than the
> multiplication table.[24]

And just as we learn the multiplication tables from our parents or teachers, we also learn moral truths from our parents and teachers—but that does not imply that our parents and teachers *invented* these moral truths.

Some people argue that our moral sense is instilled in us by the society in which we live. Though that may be partially true, certain aspects of our moral understanding seem to transcend culture. Why is it, for example, that even as outsiders to the Iraqi culture, we intuitively judged as wrong the actions of Saddam Hussein when we learned that he had murdered family members, tortured and killed people he considered to be political threats, and ordered the gassing of thousands of Kurds? Whether or not one supported military actions to stop him, we knew that what he had done to his own people was wrong—period.

And Adolf Hitler? His "final solution" to eliminate the Jewish race may have emanated from his own heartless insanity, but it was soon embraced by many others—not only the leaders but the entire Nazi party and its supporters. Yet we do not, and certainly should not, hold back from condemning the Nazis' horrible actions merely because what they did was within the context of their own culture or in line with their own laws.

At the Nuremberg trials after the war, people both inside and outside German society stepped up and judged what had been done within the Nazi culture based on a universal sense of morality. And rightly so. If murdering innocent people is wrong in your own home, certainly it is wrong in your neighbor's home across the street or on the other side of town—and in other countries where they speak different languages. It doesn't matter where one commits murder; it's still wrong.

Yet, where did we get this sense of right and wrong? If we didn't invent it, if it transcends the realms of culture and politics, if it's something we can't get away from, then what is its source? Could it be that a *Moral Lawgiver* actually knit those moral standards, along with the ability to understand and operate by them, into the very fabric of what it means to be human?

Could it be that a Moral Lawgiver *actually knit those moral standards into the very fabric of what it means to be human?*

That conclusion certainly seems to square with logic and experience. Interestingly, it's also in line with what the Bible tells us: "They demonstrate that God's law is written in their hearts, for their own conscience and thoughts either accuse them or tell them they are doing right."[25]

The "moral argument" is summed up well by Lee Strobel in *The Case for Faith*:

> Without God, morality is simply the product of sociobiological
> evolution and basically a question of taste or personal
> preference. . . . Without God, there is no absolute right and
> wrong that imposes itself on our conscience. But we know

deep down that objective moral values *do* exist—some actions, like rape and child torture, for example, are universal moral abominations—and, therefore, this means God exists.[26]

Our sense of morality really does imply the existence of a *Moral Lawgiver.*

∞

Though much more could be said, and many more arguments could be given from the logical and scientific realms, the evidence from these points alone aims strongly toward a *Divine Being* who began this immense universe with a bang; who shaped it and all of the creatures in it with incredible detail and design; who fine-tuned it to extremely precise tolerances so it would be able to support life, including yours and mine; who encoded our DNA with an amazingly complex and comprehensive language; and who created us as humans with a pervasive and inescapable sense of morality.

Add it all up, and it seems highly advisable to choose a faith that takes these facts into account by honoring that Divine Being in appropriate ways.

CHAPTER TEN

"HOW CAN I *FIGURE OUT* WHAT TO BELIEVE?"

Part 2: Considering the Textual Criteria

THAT WHICH WAS FROM THE BEGINNING,
WHICH WE HAVE HEARD, WHICH WE HAVE SEEN
WITH OUR EYES, WHICH WE HAVE LOOKED AT AND
OUR HANDS HAVE TOUCHED—THIS WE PROCLAIM
CONCERNING THE WORD OF LIFE.

1 John 1:1 (NIV)

In chapter 9, we explored some of the logical and scientific reasons that point toward the existence of a wise and powerful God—a God who is the cause of the universe and the designer who shaped it to support life. We saw how he also wove his moral standards into the fabric of the human personality, causing us to be aware of the sobering reality that we all fall short of that benchmark.

In this chapter, we'll examine whether the Bible can be considered a reliable text on which to base our faith.

Arrow 6 ····⟩ The Bible shows itself to be a uniquely *consistent* religious book.

Despite a growing number of attacks on the Bible in recent years, it still stands strong as a testimony to its own supernatural composition. How? One way is through its extraordinary *consistency*.

People often talk about the Bible as if it were one book, but it is actually a collection of many books. Yet these documents show amazing unity, as noted by scholars Norman Geisler and William Nix:

> Composed as it is of sixty-six books, written over a period of some fifteen hundred years by about forty authors using several languages and containing hundreds of topics, it is more than accidental or incidental that the Bible possesses an amazing unity of theme—*Jesus Christ.*[1]
>
> It is only later reflection, both by the prophets themselves (for example, see 1 Peter 1:10-11) and later generations, that has discovered that the Bible is really one book whose "chapters" were written by men who had no explicit knowledge of the overall structure. Their individual roles could be compared to that of different men writing chapters of a novel for which none

of them have even an overall outline. Whatever unity the book
has must come from beyond them. Like a symphony, each
individual part of the Bible contributes to an overall unity that is
orchestrated by one Master.[2]

This degree of consistency would be difficult enough to
achieve within a single book by a solo author—but when you
add the complexity of multiple writers, from multiple countries, in multiple languages, over multiple centuries, dealing
with multiple problems and situations, the Bible's incredible co-
hesion and unified message are nothing short of miraculous.

The best way to get a sense of this
is to spend some time reading the Bible
for yourself, preferably in an easily read-
able version like the New Living Translation.[3] As you read, look for logical
consistency, experiential relevance, and
the subjective-but-real "ring of truth"
that countless people have affirmed
over the years. I believe you'll find this
as you read.

*As you read, look for
logical consistency,
experiential relevance,
and the subjective-but-
real "ring of truth" that
countless people have
affirmed over the years.*

By contrast, it's worth pointing
out that this high level of consistency
is absent from later would-be gospels
that some scholars claim should have been part of the biblical canon.[4] For example, after you've spent some time reading
the ennobling but challenging insights of Jesus in the biblical
Gospels, contrast them to what is probably the most famous
of the so-called Gnostic gospels, the Gospel of Thomas, which
came along more than a century later:

Jesus is quoted in Saying 14 of Thomas as telling his disciples:
"If you fast, you will bring sin upon yourselves, and if you pray,
you will be condemned, and if you give to charity, you will
harm your spirits." He is quoted in Saying 114 as teaching that
"every female who makes herself male will enter the kingdom
of Heaven." The gospel also quotes Jesus in Saying 7 as offering
this inscrutable insight: "Blessings on the lion if a human eats
it, making the lion human. Foul is the human if a lion eats it,
making the lion human."[5]

Does that make sense to you? If your reaction is anything
like mine, you're probably ready to get back to the real Jesus of
history, as described in the genuine Gospels of Matthew, Mark,
Luke, and John. I think it's clear that the biblical Gospels, along
with the other documents in the Bible, have the earmarks of
truth because of their matchless clarity and consistency.

Arrow 7 ⋯⋙ The Bible is a uniquely *historical* religious book.

The accounts in the Bible, particularly those in the New Testament, are based mostly on direct, eyewitness testimony. For
example, the apostle John wrote, "That which was from the
beginning, which we have heard, which we have seen with our
eyes, which we have looked at and our hands have touched—
this we proclaim."[6] Other parts of the New Testament were
compiled by writers who interacted with various eyewitnesses.
This includes careful and conscientious historians like Luke,
who made a point of explaining his research methodology:
"Many people have set out to write accounts about the events
that have been fulfilled among us. They used the eyewitness
reports circulating among us from the early disciples. Having

carefully investigated everything from the beginning, I also have decided to write a careful account . . . so you can be certain of the truth of everything you were taught."[7]

These accounts also were written down early—soon after the events they chronicle and easily within the lifespan of the people who walked with Jesus. I mention this because there are still some outdated rumors circulating that say the New Testament Gospels were penned at a much later time. One of the early proponents of that theory, theologian John A. T. Robinson, did additional research and made a dramatic turnaround. In fact, he later repudiated his previous claims and wrote a book titled *Redating the New Testament,* which corrected what he and others had been teaching.[8] In it, Robinson argues that the entire New Testament was written before AD 70. (To put this in context, the date of Jesus' resurrection is widely believed to

These accounts also were written down early—soon after the events they chronicle and easily within the lifespan of the people who walked with Jesus.

have been in AD 30 or 33.) But even if the last part of the New Testament was written a bit later—say closer to AD 90, as many scholars believe, it's clear that the entire New Testament was completed within a generation of Christ's death and resurrection. That means there were many people still living who could vouch for its accuracy.

To put this in a modern perspective, most of the New Testament would have been completed within a span of years similar to the time that has elapsed since the assassination of John F. Kennedy (1963), the first visit of the Beatles to America (1964), and the first time a man walked on the moon (1969)—events that are vividly remembered by many of us today. And even the latest books would have been written within a span of years comparable to the time that has elapsed since the modern state of Israel was founded (1948), again well within the lifespan and memory of many people alive today. And, obviously, if somebody now tried to rewrite history about any of those modern events, it would be quickly detected and refuted.[9] But we have no record of any contemporaries of the New Testament writers trying to factually challenge what had been written, which gives further confirmation that it was true.

The historical nature of the New Testament is also confirmed by a subsequent line of disciples who wrote and affirmed what had been taught from the beginning, including the early church fathers Polycarp, Ignatius, and Clement. Moreover, various details of the New Testament claims are reinforced by early outside reports, such as those by Thallus, Roman historians Tacitus and Suetonius, the Jewish historian Josephus, and a number of others.[10]

It's interesting to contrast the Bible to other religious writings, such as the Quran. Muslims generally grant that the Quran does not claim to be a historical book as much as a book of religious laws. Even so, it makes detailed claims about Jesus' life and teachings based on Muhammad's writings six hundred years later and six hundred miles from the scene. (These claims are contradicted by eyewitness accounts written by people who were actually with Jesus and who wrote firsthand biographies about him.) We can also compare the Bible to the *Book of Mormon*, which is based on golden tablets that Joseph Smith allegedly dug up near his home in Manchester, New York, and translated into English before they were whisked away by an angel (these writings contain many claims that are not supported by either history or archaeology); or to Hindu writings, which largely don't make historical claims at all.[11] When you do these sorts of comparisons, the Bible really shines as a book of impressive historical credential.

Arrow 8 ┄┄> The Bible is a uniquely *preserved* work of antiquity.

It is an oft-repeated objection: "You can't trust the Bible—it's been translated and retranslated so many times that you can no longer rely on anything it says." If you've ever heard that objection, you can forget about it. Anyone who says this simply doesn't know the facts.

The Bible we have today is not the end of some long chain of translations from one language to the next—say, from Greek to Latin, then Latin to German, then German to English, and so on. Rather, it is based on direct translations into English from early historical manuscripts in the original languages: Hebrew for the Old Testament and Greek for the New Testament. Every good translation goes back to the earliest documents and, based on two thousand years of linguistic and cultural studies, puts what was written there into accurate contemporary language. The result is that we can easily read and understand what was originally written in Hebrew or Greek by the prophets and apostles.[12]

The Bible we have today is based on direct translations into English from early historical manuscripts in the original languages.

Also, for the New Testament, we have literally thousands of early Greek manuscripts or partial manuscripts (and about twenty thousand more in other languages).[13] As is the case with all ancient writings, we don't have the original handwritten documents themselves (called the *autographs*), but we do have many reliable copies.

What makes the New Testament really stand out is that we have so many *more* copies than we have for any other ancient work, and they are so much *earlier* (in other words, dating closer to the time of the original writing). For example, we have 650 copies of Homer's *Iliad* (which is the highest number for any ancient writing outside of the Bible), the earliest of which was recorded a full *one thousand years* after the original.[14] Compare this to the more than five thousand manuscripts or manuscript fragments we have of the Greek New Testament— including some that can be dated to within just a few decades (and possibly even a few years) of the original writing.

Much more typical of ancient works is Caesar's *Gallic Wars*, of which we have only ten manuscripts, the earliest dating to about one thousand years after the original. Then there are the writings of Tacitus, of which we have a total of about twenty full or partial copies, with a time gap between their origins and the earliest copies of about 1,100 years.[15] Yet these historical works are all considered reliable. That being the case, when you consider the thousands of New Testament manuscripts, and a "time gap" that is so amazingly small, *there really is no comparison*.

Also, because we have thousands of New Testament manuscripts, we can compare them and study them to determine to an amazing degree of accuracy what was originally written. Some critics today are trying to make the differences between these copies seem like a big problem. But the truth is that the differences are mostly insignificant, and none of them affects any important teachings or doctrines. Although it's true that having more copies makes for more variations between those copies, it's also true that we have a much greater opportunity to ascertain the original message with much greater accuracy. Compare the New Testament to the writings of Plato, for example, of which we have only seven copies. When there's a variance among those seven copies, it's a much bigger guess to figure out which version to trust.

John Ankerberg described the situation on one of his television broadcasts:

> Suppose we had a classroom of fifty high school seniors and we asked them to hand copy the Declaration of Independence. The "A" students would make very few errors; the "B" students perhaps a few more; the "C" students a fair number—and my friends would make a lot! But if we compared them all, we could easily reconstruct what the Declaration of Independence says.[16]

If that illustration has power with just fifty high school students of varying abilities and motivation levels, how much more does it show the overwhelming accuracy of more than five thousand manuscripts copied by people whose lives were all about the message they were seeking to preserve?

Sir Frederic Kenyon, British scholar and former director of the London Museum, summed it up well when he said, "The last foundation for any doubt that the Scriptures have come down to us substantially as they were written has now been removed. Both the authenticity and the general integrity of the books of the New Testament may be regarded as finally established."[17]

More recently, and with full awareness of some of the recent attacks on the integrity of the biblical text, Daniel B. Wallace, coauthor of the incisive book *Reinventing Jesus*, summarized the situation in an interview with Lee Strobel:

> The quantity and quality of the New Testament manuscripts are unequaled in the ancient Greco-Roman world. The average Greek author has fewer than twenty copies of his works still in existence, and they come from no sooner than five hundred to a thousand years later. If you stacked the copies of his works on top of each other, they would be about four feet tall. Stack up copies of the New Testament and they would reach more than a mile high.[18]

That's a long way of saying that the English-language translations of the Bible available to us today are an accurate and trustworthy rendition of the original biblical texts— and we can read them with confidence.

Arrow 9 ⋯⋗ Archaeology shows the Bible to be a powerfully *verified* book.

In an earlier chapter, I showed how one disputed fact—the existence of the Hittite people described in the Old Testament—was clearly answered through archaeological research that strongly confirmed the Bible's assertion. This same pattern has been repeated literally thousands of times as various cities, nations, leaders, kings, languages, customs, and events mentioned in the Bible—which had previously been doubted by scholars—have been substantiated through the discovery and analysis of various artifacts.[19]

Sir William Ramsay, one of the great archaeologists of the late nineteenth and early twentieth century, started out as a staunch skeptic, doubting many details recorded in the New Testament. But then he spent thirty years of his life tracking down and confirming example after example of claims made in the Gospel of Luke, as well as in Luke's second work, the book of Acts. Here's what Ramsay finally conceded: "Luke is a historian of the first rank. . . . This author should be placed along with the very greatest of historians."[20]

Renowned archaeologist Nelson Glueck, who was once featured on the cover of *Time* magazine, said, "No archaeological discovery has ever controverted a single biblical reference. Scores of archaeological findings have been made which confirm in clear outline or exact detail historical statements in the Bible. And, by the same token, proper evaluation of biblical descriptions has often led to amazing discoveries."[21]

Events mentioned in the Bible—which had previously been doubted by scholars—have been substantiated through the discovery and analysis of various artifacts.

Another of the world's great archaeologists, William F. Albright, declared, "All radical schools in New Testament criticism which have existed in the past or which exist today are pre-archeological, and are therefore, since they were built in *der Luft* [in the air], quite antiquated today."[22]

The bottom line from an archaeological perspective: Don't bet against the Bible. Time and again, it has proven to be trustworthy in even its incidental details—which gives us confidence that its reporting of more important matters is equally accurate.

Arrow 10 ⤏ The Bible shows itself to be a uniquely *honest* religious book.

I include this point because of an idea some critics have perpetuated over the years that Christianity is all about wish fulfillment.

The theory is that people wanted a religion that would make them feel better, so they projected a Heavenly Father into the sky and started pretending he actually existed.[23] Then they invented all kinds of additional myths and stories about virgin births, miracles, and resurrections to go with it.

Here's a major problem with this theory: The Bible contains a lot of sobering information that in no way fits what people would make up if they were inventing a religion.

For example, from time to time the God of the Bible gets tired of people's disobedience, so he brings punishment on people—not only his enemies but sometimes even his friends, and occasionally in ways that seem abrupt and harsh. This God declares that he will ultimately judge those who persist in their rebelliousness toward him, allowing them to "go their own way" not only in this life, but eventually all the way into eternity—to a place of lasting separation that he labeled with a very unpopular title: *Hell*.

The Bible is brutally honest about the ethical and moral failures of some of its key characters, including some of its own writers.

Now, you may or may not agree with what the Bible teaches, but don't accuse Christians of making these things up to soothe their minds or to try to make everyone feel better. These are not feel-good, fairy-tale concepts. The book of Proverbs says, "Faithful are the wounds of a friend; but the kisses of an enemy are deceitful."[24] The Bible sometimes conveys some very serious "wounds."

The Bible is also brutally honest about the ethical and moral failures of some of its key characters, including some of its own writers. This honesty goes against a natural, built-in human aversion to casting ourselves in a negative light—yet the writers of the Bible vulnerably tell it the way it happened. Surely they wouldn't bring up these frank, humiliating, and often self-incriminating examples unless they were highly committed to reporting the real truth.

Even the core message of the Bible—that we all have corrupted hearts that lead us into all kinds of moral failure and turn us into spiritually bankrupt people who desperately need to be rescued—is not the stuff of religious happy talk. I know it's not the script *I* would have written.

These negative, but realistic, elements add up to something positive that has been called "the criterion of embarrassment"— which means that their inclusion is actually a sign of the Bible's reliability as a trustworthy historical record. The Bible's honesty also undergirds the authenticity of its claim to being a book that communicates life-giving truth from God.

Arrow 11 ⋯⟩ *Miracles*, performed in the presence of believers and critics alike, point to the prophets, apostles, and Jesus as messengers of God.

Up to this point, I've largely argued that the Bible is a historically reliable book that has been tested and proven in a variety of ways. I'm confident that this is true and that the Bible will continue to withstand the attacks being leveled at it. But what gets interesting is that, as a credible historical record, the Bible reports events that are only explainable through supernatural means: events, for example, such as miracles. Now, some people immediately write off claims of the miraculous. When asked why, they'll say, "They're impossible" or, "They would be breaking the laws of nature, and that simply can't happen."

Let me offer a few thoughts:

- Many miracles are natural events timed in supernatural ways—thus, they do not break any laws of nature. An example would be the time when Jesus was in a boat during an intense storm, and he stretched out his hand to calm the wind and the waves. A storm ending is nothing out of the ordinary—all storms eventually subside. But when it happens immediately upon Jesus' command, that's something miraculous.

- It might be good to rethink what a "law of nature" is. These "laws" are not inviolable principles, recorded in the sky somewhere, by which all natural things must forever abide—or else! Rather, they are generalizations or patterns based on observations; they're descriptive, not prescriptive. They talk about the way things normally happen, not the way they must happen. But if God set things up to go the way they usually do, it should be no problem for him, the ultimate cause of the universe, to do something a bit different now and then. In fact, if he is a creative, powerful, and wise God, then stopping storms, causing a virgin to bear a son, healing the sick, and even raising the dead would all be mere child's play to him.

- Beware of making up your mind before you see the actual evidence. Otherwise, you're exhibiting classic, closed-minded prejudice (which literally means to "pre-judge"), which might preclude you from seeing or experiencing something authentically supernatural. Instead, find out what the witnesses actually saw; what made them think it was real; whether the witnesses agree on the essential details; whether they tested it or thought about it critically; whether they're sticking with their story over the long haul; how the critics reacted, and what kinds of evidence they brought against it; whether any of them changed their minds based on what they saw or learned, and so forth. Open your mind, investigate carefully, and let the evidence guide you.

What's interesting about Jesus' miracles is that they were not contested by his enemies. The signs themselves were too obviously real—so instead his critics would try to catch him on a technicality. "Sure, you healed the man," they would say, "but you did it on the Sabbath day, which is a big no-no." But don't miss the fact that their accusations were actually admissions that he'd done something miraculous. Otherwise, what were they accusing him of?

What's interesting about Jesus' miracles is that they were not contested by his enemies. The signs themselves were too obviously real.

So, again, my advice is to read the biblical accounts for yourself, with your mind receptive to learning what actually happened, rather than being dead set against what you "*know* could not have happened." When you approach the historical accounts with an open mind, I think you'll see some exciting new doors of understanding begin to open.

Arrow 12 ····⟩ *Fulfilled prophecies* point to the Bible as a divinely inspired book and to Jesus as the unique Messiah of God.

Here is a well-known Bible verse: "All of us, like sheep, have strayed away. We have left God's paths to follow our own. Yet the LORD laid on him the sins of us all."[25]

Dr. Michael Rydelnik tells the story of what a friend of his did with this passage:

> I had a friend who typed this [Isaiah 53:6] up on his computer, without any verse notations, and took it around to everyone in his office in the motor vehicle bureau in the state capital. He said, "Just tell me who this is and where it comes from."
>
> Every single person that looked at it, Jew or Gentile alike, read it and said, "It is obviously Jesus of Nazareth, that's who it is. And it is from the New Testament."
>
> And then my friend would say, "No, it is not from the New Testament. It is from the Hebrew Bible. It was written eight centuries before Jesus came. *Can you believe this?*" And he showed it to them from Isaiah, and people really had a hard time with it. Because if you read this passage without any kind of presuppositions or bias, it will be really clear that this is the life of Yeshua (Jesus).[26]

Biblical prophecy is amazing—and the deeper you look, the more astounding it becomes. For instance, if you read Isaiah 53 in its entirety, it will be clear that the entire chapter is an amazing prophecy of the suffering of the Messiah, and it was written hundreds of years before the event. It describes, in advance, how Jesus was "pierced for our rebellion, crushed for our sins. He was beaten so we could be whole. He was whipped so we could be healed."[27]

Another prophecy, found in Zechariah 12:10, says that people will look on the one "whom they have pierced and mourn for him as for an only son. They will grieve bitterly for him as for a firstborn son who has died." It's easy to look at the crucifixion of Jesus from our side of history and see clearly how his brutal death fulfilled these prophetic words. But what really shows the divine insight in the words of these prophets is that these words were written not only hundreds of years before the life and death of Christ, but also centuries before the Roman practice of crucifixion had even been invented (with its horrific piercing of the hands and feet with nails that were pounded into the wood of the cross). I imagine that the prophets who penned these words were scratching their heads in bewilderment as they sensed God leading them to write about how the suffering Messiah would be "pierced."

If you look at the rest of that psalm, it also predicts numerous details concerning the suffering and sacrificial death of the Messiah.

It's also interesting that Jesus, while hanging on the cross, called the attention of those standing nearby to the Old Testament passage of Psalm 22. He did this by quoting the first line of the psalm, crying out, "My God, my God, why have you forsaken me?"[28] This was a standard way in that culture for teachers to focus their listeners on a particular place in the Hebrew scriptures.

If you look at the rest of that psalm, it also predicts numerous details concerning the suffering and sacrificial death of the

Messiah. Here are a few of those phrases, including yet another ancient prediction about his being pierced, but adding the astonishing detail that the piercing would be through his hands and feet. These words were penned about a thousand years before Jesus' crucifixion:

> My God, my God, why have you forsaken me? Why are you so far from saving me, so far from the words of my groaning? . . . All who see me mock me; they hurl insults, shaking their heads: "He trusts in the LORD; let the LORD rescue him." . . . I am poured out like water, and all my bones are out of joint. My heart has turned to wax; it has melted away within me. My strength is dried up like a potsherd, and my tongue sticks to the roof of my mouth; you lay me in the dust of death. . . . A band of evil men has encircled me, they have pierced my hands and my feet. I can count all my bones; people stare and gloat over me. They divide my garments among them and cast lots for my clothing.[29]

If you read about the Crucifixion as it is recorded in the Gospels (for example in Matthew 27), it is mind-boggling how these centuries-old predictions were fulfilled in such minute detail. Could any mere human have written such specific history in advance? It seems clear that God's foreknowledge was on display in these predictions—and we've only mentioned a few of the many examples that could be discussed. Others include the place of the Messiah's birth being in Bethlehem (Micah 5:2); his being of the lineage of King David (2 Samuel 7:12-16); his being born of a virgin (Isaiah 7:14); his claim of deity (Isaiah 9:6); his rejection by his own people (Isaiah 53:3); his betrayal for thirty pieces of silver (Zechariah 11:12); his extreme suffering and disfigurement

(Isaiah 52:14); his death on our behalf (Isaiah 53:5-6); his burial in a rich man's tomb (Isaiah 53:9); and his subsequent resurrection (Psalm 16:10). Many other examples could be listed, though these are some of the most prominent.

Obviously, Jesus (if he were merely human) could not manipulate circumstances in order to intentionally fulfill these predictions. And the odds of these prophecies all being fulfilled by one person are vanishingly small. "Someone did the math and figured out that the probability of just eight [messianic] prophecies being fulfilled is one chance in one hundred million billion. That number is millions of times greater than the total number of people who've ever walked the planet."[30]

It is mind-boggling how these centuries-old predictions were fulfilled in such minute detail. It seems clear that God's foreknowledge was on display in these predictions.

I won't trouble you with the number of zeroes it would take to represent the odds of *forty-eight* messianic prophecies being fulfilled by one person. Just trust me when I tell you it would make your brain ache.[31]

Just a few days after his resurrection, Jesus walked along a road with two of his followers who were trying to understand the events of Jesus' crucifixion. At first, they were prevented from recognizing him as he admonished them with these words: "You foolish people! You find it so hard to believe all that the prophets wrote in the Scriptures. Wasn't it clearly predicted that the Messiah would have to suffer all these things before entering his glory?"[32] Then Jesus explained to these men everything the Hebrew scriptures said about him.

It wasn't until a bit later, just after Jesus had left them, that the two men realized it had actually been Jesus. In awe they said to each other, "Didn't our hearts burn within us as he talked with us on the road and explained the Scriptures to us?"[33]

For me, these prophecies, along with the records of miracles we discussed in the last point, serve as further reasons to trust the Bible, not only as an accurate historical book but also as one that is divinely inspired and therefore uniquely suited to guide us in choosing our faith.

CHAPTER ELEVEN

"HOW CAN I *FIGURE OUT* WHAT TO BELIEVE?"

Part 3: Considering the Historical and Experiential Criteria

THE DOORS WERE LOCKED; BUT SUDDENLY, AS BEFORE,
JESUS WAS STANDING AMONG THEM. "PEACE BE
WITH YOU," HE SAID. THEN HE SAID TO THOMAS,
"PUT YOUR FINGER HERE, AND LOOK AT MY HANDS.
PUT YOUR HAND INTO THE WOUND IN MY SIDE.
DON'T BE FAITHLESS ANY LONGER. BELIEVE!"
"MY LORD AND MY GOD!" THOMAS EXCLAIMED.
THEN JESUS TOLD HIM, "YOU BELIEVE BECAUSE
YOU HAVE SEEN ME. BLESSED ARE THOSE WHO
BELIEVE WITHOUT SEING ME."

John 20:26-29

In this chapter, we'll explore the historical and experiential realms, looking at a number of additional "arrows" in the broader arsenal of information that supports not only the existence of a *theistic* God, but more specifically, the God of the Christian faith.

Arrow 13 ····⟩ Jesus' *sinless life* backed up his claim to be the Son of God.

In an age when so many religious leaders talk a good game but fail to live up to their own press releases, it's a huge relief to find out that nobody ever found fault with Jesus—for *anything*. That included his closest companions, who would have easily picked out any character flaws, moral or ethical inconsistencies, or even old-fashioned human error and frailty.* But nothing was detected or reported in terms of defects or weaknesses—not even from Jesus' own mother, who certainly would have known.

This is important, not because a leader needs to be perfect in order to be followed, but because Jesus claimed repeatedly to be the Son of God. If that claim was true, it would certainly require that he be sinless and without flaw.

Throughout the four Gospels, we frequently see Jesus' enemies trying to catch him doing something—anything—wrong. But even they were left quibbling over peripheral details, like whether Jesus kept certain obscure rules to the letter of the law. And in the end, these opponents were the ones who had to hire false witnesses to invent stories in order to try to accuse Jesus of wrongdoing. Knowing as they did that none of it was true,

---

*Philosophy professor Dallas Willard once made an interesting observation. He said that one of the best evidences for Jesus' deity is that he spent about three years on a camping trip with twelve men, and when it was over, eleven of them still followed him as Messiah and Lord.

you can imagine their frustration when at one point Jesus even threw the reality of his sinless life back in their face. "Which of you can truthfully accuse me of sin?" he asked them.[1]

When it was all said and done, the only accusation that they could make stick against Jesus was that of blasphemy—for which they ended up indicting him because, as it says in John 5:18, "he called God his Father, thereby making himself equal with God." And his claim to equality with the Father *would* have been blasphemy—had it not been true.

No other major religious leader ever claimed to be sinless. Muhammad was very open about his own need for God's forgiveness. In the Quran, for example, he says he was told to "patiently, then, persevere: for the Promise of Allah is true: and *ask forgiveness for thy fault*, and celebrate the Praises of thy Lord in the evening and in the morning."[2]

Joseph Smith, the founder of Mormonism, died in a gun battle as he fought to get out of jail with a six-shooter in his hand. The records show that two of the people he shot soon died from their wounds. That's in sharp contrast with Jesus, who willingly laid down his own life for his friends.

Jesus is a leader you can respect, imitate, trust, and follow in *everything*—without fear of embarrassment or recrimination. His words and actions, without exception, back up his claim to being the unique Son of God.

Arrow 14 ····⟩ Jesus' *resurrection* powerfully established his credentials as the Son of God.

Three days after his crucifixion, Jesus miraculously rose from the dead, just as he'd predicted.[3] This supernatural event has been well documented and attested to in a number of compelling ways. I'll briefly discuss three of those ways here, though the next few "arrows" further support the historic reality of the resurrection.

Jesus' tomb was empty.

Starting with the women who first visited the tomb and then the men who followed soon after, the disciples all testified that it was empty—in bewilderment at first because they didn't fully grasp what had happened. But nobody, not even the disciples' enemies, disputed the fact that the tomb was vacant. Instead, the religious authorities made up a story and bribed the guards, coaching them to say, "Jesus' disciples came during the night while we were sleeping, and they stole his body." If you reflect on this statement for just a moment, you'll realize how ridicu-

Their fabricated story does do something useful: It concedes that the tomb really was empty, and it demonstrates that the religious leaders had no idea how to explain it.

lous their story was. If the guards had really been asleep, they wouldn't have had any idea what happened to the body. On the other hand, if they had seen the disciples stealing the body, they would have stopped and arrested them. But their fabricated story *does* do something useful: It concedes that the tomb really was empty, and it demonstrates that the religious leaders had no idea how to explain it.

Let me also note that there's no good rationale for saying that anyone stole or moved the body. The *Romans*, who were ruling in Palestine at the time, wanted Jesus dead, and they crucified him. They had no interest or motivation to do anything that would make anyone think otherwise. The *Jewish leaders* wanted Jesus dead (and they wanted him to *stay* dead). If there had been a body to be found, you can bet they would have put it on display to quash the upstart movement of Christianity that was threatening their authority. The *disciples* were scared to death after the Crucifixion, and they— including Peter, who was grief stricken and full of shame after repeatedly denying Jesus during his trial—were hiding in a room somewhere trying to decide what to do next. The disciples had neither the motivation nor the means to overcome the guards, steal Jesus' body, and then—what?—make up stories and lie about it for the rest of their lives, face persecution, and end up becoming martyrs for no good reason? I don't think so. The best explanation for Jesus' empty tomb is Jesus' resurrection.

The risen Jesus was seen by eyewitnesses.

With the possible exception of John, the early disciples did not believe in the Resurrection merely based on the empty tomb—they believed in it because they saw the risen Jesus, talked to him, and even ate with him. Two leading authorities on the Resurrection, Gary Habermas and Michael Licona, write in *The Case for the Resurrection of Jesus* that "friends as well as foes saw

Thomas wouldn't believe in any resurrection claims without extremely solid evidence. But then he met the risen Jesus and saw the scars on his hands and side.

Jesus not once but many times over a period of forty days. We are told that these numbers included both men and women, hardhearted Peter and softhearted Mary Magdalene, indoors and outdoors."[4]

And let's not forget the doubting skeptic named Thomas. Maybe you can relate to him. Thomas wouldn't believe in any resurrection claims without extremely solid evidence. But then he met the risen Jesus and saw the scars on his hands and side. Convinced, Thomas got on his knees and exclaimed humbly, "My Lord and my God!"—which seems to be the appropriate response, once you realize who Jesus really is.[5]

The accounts of the risen Jesus were frequent and early.

Once the followers of Jesus realized what had happened—that he truly had conquered the grave—they immediately started telling people about it. Their reports were oral at first, but they were soon written down as well.

One of the earliest creeds of the church, which scholars believe originated within just a few years of Jesus' resurrection, is recorded by Paul in 1 Corinthians 15:3-8:

> I passed on to you what was most important and what had also been passed on to me. Christ died for our sins, just as the Scriptures said. He was buried, and he was raised from the dead on the third day, just as the Scriptures said. He was seen by Peter and then by the Twelve. After that, he was seen by more than 500 of his followers at one time, most of whom are still alive, though some have died. Then he was seen by James and later by all the apostles. Last of all . . . I also saw him.

This testimony, along with corroborating accounts in the four Gospels and other books of the New Testament, simply affirms what was well-known to Christians ever since the first Easter Sunday—and it leaves no doubt regarding the clarity these early Christ-followers had about the reality of the Resurrection. Their confidence, along with the reasons that persuaded them, assures us of the bedrock reality of the resurrection of Jesus—and, with it, the truthfulness of his claim to be the Son of God.

Arrow 15 ⤏ The *emergence of the church* points to the authenticity of its message.

It truly was an incredible turn of events. Peter had assured Jesus that he would follow him even to death, but then he denied Jesus three times that very same night. After Jesus was tortured and crucified, the defeated Peter went in fear and trembling to hide out in some first-century safe house, along with the rest of the ragtag band of dejected disciples.

Fast forward a few weeks. Now Peter and the others are out in the public square—in Jerusalem, the very city where Jesus had been crucified only a few weeks earlier—and they are boldly telling everyone who will listen about the risen Christ. And if that's not enough, Peter then storms the stage and begins to preach to this potentially hostile crowd:

> People of Israel, listen! God publicly endorsed Jesus the Nazarene by doing powerful miracles, wonders, and signs through him, as you well know. But God knew what would happen, and his prearranged plan was carried out when Jesus was betrayed. With the help of lawless Gentiles, you nailed him to a cross and killed him. But God released him from the horrors of death and raised him back to life, for death could not keep him in its grip. . . .
>
> God raised Jesus from the dead, and we are all witnesses of this. Now he is exalted to the place of highest honor in heaven, at God's right hand. . . .

> So let everyone in Israel know for certain that God has made this Jesus, whom you crucified, to be both Lord and Messiah![6]

The crowd's response? Peter's words "pierced their hearts," and they cried out and asked what they should do. Peter instructed them to "repent of your sins and turn to God, and

These events confirm that the resurrection of Jesus really did happen; the early church was confident about it—and they were willing to stake their lives on it.

be baptized in the name of Jesus Christ for the forgiveness of your sins."[7] And guess what? About three thousand people did. This was only the beginning of the rapid emergence and exponential growth of the Christian church, which has continued to this day, with Christianity becoming the largest religion in the world, with more adherents in the developing world than in the entire Western world combined.[8]

This would never have happened if Peter had not been right when he so boldly proclaimed his message about Jesus. And let's not overlook the fact that he backed up his assertions with phrases like "as you well know" and "we are all witnesses to this." This appeal to public knowledge was also used by Paul when he unflinchingly declared during one of his speeches, "King Agrippa knows about these things. I speak boldly, for I am sure these events are all familiar to him, for they were not done in a corner!"[9]

Again, these events confirm that the resurrection of Jesus really did happen; the early church was confident about it as an established fact—as well as about their entire message and mission—and they were willing to stake their lives on it. That kind of confidence has proven contagious to millions of people, including me.

Arrow 16 ┈┈> The *changed lives of early skeptics* affirmed the truth of Jesus' resurrection and the teachings of the church.

It's one thing that the friends and companions of Jesus stayed faithful to his teachings and endured against the odds. But when some who opposed the Christian message—like Saul of Tarsus, who was an active persecutor of the church—and others who were skeptical of Jesus, like his own half brother James, end up becoming Jesus' devoted disciples, well, that really says something.

Saul had been present and enthusiastically supportive of the condemnation and subsequent stoning of Stephen, a Christian disciple. The book of Acts records Stephen's valiant final speech, followed by his violent end as the first recorded martyr for Christ.[10] It also mentions specifically that "Saul was one of the witnesses, and he agreed completely with the killing of Stephen," and that he "was uttering threats with every breath and was eager to kill the Lord's followers."[11]

Saul was soon on his way to Damascus to drag back to Jerusalem any Christians he might find there. It was on that journey that the risen Jesus appeared to him, temporarily blinded him, and called him to become his follower and eventually a leader in the worldwide Christian movement.[12]

Saul, who we know much better by his post-conversion name of Paul the apostle, became a powerful proponent and missionary for the faith, developing into the world's most influential leader in the spread of the message of Jesus. He helped countless people choose faith in Christ, and then he established churches in each city around these freshly committed believers.

Far less was written about James, but he was apparently a doubter of his half brother, Jesus, as they grew up together. But, later, he was one of the people Jesus visited after his resurrection (James is mentioned by name in an early creed recorded in 1 Corinthians 15), and he ended up becoming a key leader in the early church.

These two skeptics-turned-star-witnesses serve notice to the world, and to us as we consider and weigh the Christian truth claims, that this faith is built on a solid foundation of facts.

Arrow 17 ····⟫ The *willingness of the disciples to die* for claims they knew to be true affirms the trustworthiness of their claims.

We left out a very important fact about the two former skeptics we just discussed: They not only made complete turnarounds in their lives to become followers of Jesus, but they also were willing to die for the truth of their claims. This shows the level of their confidence in what they had seen and experienced, especially as witnesses of the risen Jesus.

Equally significant is the fact that almost all the other disciples—who said they saw, talked to, and ate with the risen Jesus, some of them multiple times—also died willingly as martyrs for the truth of those claims. They all refused to deny or diminish anything they had proclaimed about Jesus, his miracles, his teachings, or his resurrection.

It's fairly easy to embrace the Christian faith today, especially in our culture of freedom and tolerance. But the disciples' willingness to proclaim it in their time and culture, and eventually to die for it, provides a huge exclamation point to the reality that they really knew and believed in what they confidently proclaimed.

Some people have tried to discredit the importance of this argument by equating the disciples, and their willingness to give up their lives for what they knew to be true, with members of other religions who have died for their faith. The most common example is Muslim terrorists, such as the ones who gave up their lives to fly airplanes into the World Trade Center and the Pentagon on September 11, 2001. The argument is that they, too, were willing to die for what they believed.

But there is a major difference between these examples: The disciples of Jesus had been in a position *to know for certain* whether or not what they taught was correct. They were either telling the truth about being with the risen Savior or they were lying—but either way they knew what had really happened. So if

The disciples of Jesus were either telling the truth about being with the risen Savior or they were lying—but either way they knew what had really happened.

Jesus didn't really rise from the dead, then they knew they were lying about seeing him and went ahead and gave their lives for that lie anyway.

But who would do that? Who would say to themselves and to each other, "We know this resurrection didn't really happen; we know we're going to have to lie about it for the rest of our lives, acting in complete disobedience to all Jesus taught us about telling the truth; we know we're going to be persecuted and probably die for this lie; we know we've got nothing to gain and everything to lose; we know we'll never be able to respect ourselves or look each other in the eye again; we know that the religion we're inventing will be a complete sham; we know we'll be judged eventually by God for all of this; and we know we don't have to do this. But we're going to get our stories together (more or less) and tell them to the ends of the earth anyway. We're all going to give the same false report—all the way to prison or until we die as we stand united for this myth. *Is everybody in?*"

Can you imagine it? I can't. What would have been the upside? The real truth is this: *Nobody dies for what they know to be a lie.*

Instead, the disciples' eventual deaths, which were the result of resolutely holding to their claims to have seen the resurrected Jesus, speak *volumes* about the truthfulness of those claims. And if they were willing to die for what they knew, we ought to take it very seriously.

Their willingness to give up everything to remain faithful to what they had seen and experienced should give us confidence in these things as well.

The Muslim terrorists, on the other hand, were not in a position to verify or know anything for certain. In other words, they had been *taught* that their impending crimes were Allah's will for them and that their deaths would ensure their immediate access into paradise, but there was no way for them to test those teachings. So these men yielded to the authority of their extremist teachers, took a blind leap of faith, and gave up their lives for what they could only hope against hope—and against reason—was really God's will.

But because they had no way of evidentially affirming what they'd been promised, neither their deaths nor those of any others in this state of blind submission do anything to prove the truthfulness of their religion.

See the difference? The claims of Christianity are bolstered by the sacrifices and deaths of those who were there at the beginning and who knew for certain whether it all happened the way they said it did. Their certitude, along with their willingness to give up everything to remain faithful to what they had seen and experienced, should give us confidence in these things as well.

Arrow 18 ····⟫ The *changed minds of many modern skeptics* further support the Christian truth claims.

This arrow illustrates a different kind of reason for believing than the turnaround of the early skeptics. Their change of mind points primarily to the validity of their experience with the risen Christ. However, the conversion of modern skeptics points more to the strength of the evidence (including the "arrows" in this book) available to all of us today. Here are a few of many possible examples we could talk about:

Simon Greenleaf was a Jewish scholar and one of two professors who built the Harvard Law School into a world-class institution. He also wrote the standard textbook on what constitutes good arguments in a court of law, the three-volume *Treatise on the Law of Evidence*. So brilliant was this work that the *London Law Magazine* once declared that through it "more light has shone from the New World than from all the lawyers who adorn the courts of Europe."[13] Professor Greenleaf was challenged one day by some of his students to examine the evidence for the resurrection of Christ. Skeptical at first, he thoroughly investigated and ended up becoming an ardent follower of Jesus. He later wrote a defense of the Christian faith called *The Testimony of the Evangelists: The Gospels Examined by the Rules of Evidence.*[14]

A. H. Ross, an English journalist who set out to publish a popular book exposing the myth of the Resurrection, ended up writing a book he had not intended. Using the pen name "Frank Morison," Ross initially titled his book *The Book That Refused to be Written*, but later changed it to *Who Moved the Stone?* As the name of this now-classic book indicates, Ross's studies convinced him—initially against his will—that Jesus really did rise from the dead. Once he was convinced of that, Ross chose the Christian faith as his own and began telling others what he had discovered.

Sir Lionel Luckhoo was listed in the 1990 *Guinness Book of Records* as the world's most successful lawyer. His amazing record as a defense attorney was 245 successive murder acquittals, either before a jury or on appeal. This brilliant barrister, twice knighted by Queen Elizabeth, rigorously analyzed the evidence for the resurrection of Jesus for several years before coming to the following conclusion: "I say unequivocally that the evidence for the Resurrection of Jesus Christ is so overwhelming that it compels acceptance by proof which leaves absolutely no room for doubt."[15]

Countless other stories could be told, including that of Josh McDowell, who as a college student set out to disprove Christianity and ended up becoming a believer. McDowell wrote *More Than a Carpenter*, a great little book about the evidence for Christ that has now sold more than ten million copies, and the encyclopedic *Evidence That Demands a Verdict*, which presents further evidence for the truth of Christianity.[16] And then there's the story of Viggo Olsen, who, as a medical student with a promising future as a surgeon, took a challenge from his wife's parents to examine the evidence for Christianity. What he thought would be a brief investigation turned into a life-changing spiritual quest. In the end, both Viggo and his wife, Joan, came to faith in Jesus. They subsequently spent thirty-three years as medical missionaries to the poor in Bangladesh.[17] And there's my close friend and ministry partner, Lee Strobel, who as the skeptical legal editor for the *Chicago Tribune* investigated Christianity for nearly two years before finding faith. Today, Lee speaks and writes about the

The fact that so many smart people have carefully investigated the facts and ended up choosing the Christian faith doesn't necessarily make it true.

kinds of evidence that convinced him, which he describes in his best sellers *The Case for Christ, The Case for Faith, The Case for a Creator,* and *The Case for the Real Jesus.*

The fact that so many smart people have carefully investigated the facts and ended up choosing the Christian faith doesn't necessarily make it true—but it certainly lends weight to that possibility. At a minimum, it seems it should motivate any sincere seeker to consider the points of evidence that have convinced so many other serious thinkers.

Arrow 19 ····⟩ **The *testimonies of countless believers* throughout history attest to the reality of God and the value of following Jesus.**

In addition to the logical reasons and various points of evidence we've discussed, consider the fact that millions of people, from extremely diverse backgrounds, cultures, and walks of life—along the corridors of time—have found that faith in Jesus makes a significant difference in their daily lives as well as in their outlook for the future.

I certainly know that my life is better because of God's guidance and wisdom, even if applied imperfectly. Over and over, God's ways, as revealed in the Bible, have proven themselves. When I've carefully sought God's will and direction, they have consistently proven to be what's best for me. This is true not only in the spiritual realm, but also in the relational, marital, and vocational areas of my life. For me, choosing to place my faith in Jesus has proven to be the best way to live—and I'm confident that someday it will also show itself to be the only way to die.

Arrow 20 ⋯⋗ It's true because *Jesus said so*—and he has the credentials to speak with authority.

Have you ever noticed that almost everyone tries to claim Jesus, in one way or another, as being their very own?

To the social activist, he's a cultural revolutionary; to the metaphysical New Ager, he's an enlightened spiritual master; to the Baha'i, he's one of many great prophets; to the liberal, he's another liberal; to the extreme fundamentalist, he's an angry street preacher; to the Unitarian, he's a universalist; to the corporate executive, he's the consummate business leader; to the Communist, he's the head of a commune; to the motivational teacher, he's the ultimate positive thinker; to postmodernists, he's different things, depending on their various perspectives; and to the irreverent coworker, he's simply "the guy upstairs."

To our natural way of thinking, Jesus is everybody's buddy—and in almost every case, our image of him ends up looking suspiciously like ourselves. Someone quipped, "In the beginning, God created human beings in his own image—and then we quickly returned him the favor." It's both funny and strange how one side of our brain desperately longs for a God who is transcendently exalted and high above us, and then the other side of our brain does everything it can to try to pull God down to our own mundane level.

To our natural way of thinking, Jesus is everybody's buddy—and in almost every case, our image of him ends up looking suspiciously like ourselves.

In spite of all of this, I'd like to make a modest proposal: Why don't we let Jesus speak for himself? After all, he has credentials like nobody else. Of all the people who have walked this planet, he was the best at communicating what he wanted to say—sometimes with challenging words and often with encouraging ones.

Here are some of his challenging words that we'd be wise to pay heed to:

"I am the way, the truth, and the life. No one can come to the Father except through me."[18]

"You will know the truth, and the truth will set you free."[19]

And here are some of his encouraging words:

"Come to me, all of you who are weary and carry heavy burdens, and I will give you rest. Take my yoke upon you. Let me teach you, because I am humble and gentle at heart, and you will find rest for your souls. For my yoke is easy to bear, and the burden I give you is light."[20]

In the next two chapters, we'll look at what all those reasons mean, as well as what we should consider doing about it. But first let me conclude this three-chapter section of reasons for the Christian faith with this wise word of admonition from Simon Greenleaf, the distinguished Harvard lawyer I mentioned earlier: "In examining the evidences of the Christian religion, it is essential to the discovery of truth that we bring to the investigation a mind freed, as far as possible, from existing prejudice, and open to conviction. There should be a readiness, on our part, to investigate with candor, to follow the truth wherever it may lead us, and to submit, without reserve or objection, to all the teachings of this religion, if it be found to be of divine origin."[21]

"I'D *LIKE* TO HAVE FAITH"

Breaking through the Barriers to Belief

TRUTH IS SO OBSCURE IN THESE TIMES AND
FALSEHOOD SO ESTABLISHED THAT UNLESS ONE
LOVES THE TRUTH, HE CANNOT KNOW IT.

Blaise Pascal

I went mountain biking this morning—actually,
just moments ago. The weather was ideal: sunshine
with a cool breeze. The trail winds through the can-
yons in the foothills near our home. The scenery

is stunning with views of the higher mountains off in the distance and occasional glimpses of the Pacific Ocean out beyond the valleys. Sometimes I find myself peddling down the path chasing a roadrunner (*Beep! Beep!* Don't worry; I'm no threat to those speedsters), and I often see deer and scare up a variety of other interesting animals. I love the aroma of sage and other fragrant bushes, flowers, and trees as I go blazing by them.

I'm sorry to mar that idyllic image, but I should also mention that people sometimes get seriously injured while biking these trails. There are plenty of boulders, washouts, and cliffs that can send a rider unexpectedly airborne. Mechanical failure of the bike can also cause catastrophic crashes, like the one I heard about recently when the rider's handlebars collapsed as he landed a jump. There are also poisonous insects and reptiles, as my friend Chris will attest—he was bitten last month by a rattlesnake.

And then there are the mountain lions.

I thought that they were sort of a joke when I first moved to the area—until I heard about a mountain biker who was killed by one about ten miles from where I ride. Later that same day, a woman was mauled by the same angry cougar. More recently, a lion was shot in the backyard of some people who live a few blocks from me, and this summer another one was spotted at night walking along our street!

I had figured that because I ride fast I was probably safe. But I did a little research and learned that these cats—which can weigh up to 170 pounds and measure eight feet long from nose to tail—can run forty miles per hour, jump twenty feet straight into the air and up into a tree, and apparently are attracted to faster-moving prey, just like kittens are drawn to rolling balls of yarn.

Now I carry a knife and a cell phone whenever I ride (the state doesn't allow sawed-off shotguns), neither of which would probably help me, but at least I feel as if I've taken *some* precaution. It's not as if you can go out and buy mountain lion repellent.

The bottom line is this: To at least some degree, *I ride by faith*. I don't *know* that I'm going to be safe or come home in one piece, but the evidence and the odds weigh in my favor. In fact, statistically it's about as unlikely to get killed by a mountain lion as it is to die of a shark attack—and the chances of either one are about 1/100 of the likelihood of being killed by lightning and 1/50,000 of the chance of dying in an automobile accident.[1] So, if you ever go outside where you could possibly be struck by lightning—or, worse yet, if you're crazy enough to ever ride in a car—then *you live by faith much more than I do* when I'm riding my mountain bike.

That's just the way life is. We pursue our normal, daily activities with faith that they'll work out for the best—like they did yesterday. There's no proof or absolute assurance that this will actually be the case, but we work from the information we have and live our lives anyway.

> *That's just the way life is. We pursue our normal, daily activities with faith that they'll work out for the best—like they did yesterday.*

Choosing Your Faith

Wise, spiritual faith—the kind I'm advocating—is a commitment of trust based on solid, though incomplete, evidence that we're believing in the right things and moving in the best direction. This understanding of *faith*, I should point out, is in sharp contrast to the fuzzy and often misguided definitions we see floating about in contemporary culture. Here are a few examples of those:

- *Wishful thinking,* in the relativistic, it's-true-for-you sense, which we discussed in chapter 2 and found lacking.

- *Therapeutic faith,* which is similar to wishful thinking, but based more on comfort and emotional support. In reality it may make you feel good but still be false.

- *Unfounded belief,* also known as *blind faith,* as described by atheist Richard Dawkins: "Faith is the great cop-out, the great excuse to evade the need to think and evaluate evidence. Faith is belief in spite of, even perhaps because of, the lack of evidence. . . . Faith is not allowed to justify itself by argument."[2] My friend Erick Nelson calls this approach to faith "a kind of voluntary, self-imposed frontal lobotomy"—which certainly neither he nor I would recommend.

- *Against-the-facts faith,* an irrational approach summed up in the classic example of the Sunday School kid who defined faith by saying, "It's believing in something even though you know in your heart it couldn't possibly be true."

Contrasted to all of that, I'm advocating *reasonable faith*— which is *belief* and *action* based on *good logic* and *evidence, trustworthy revelation,* and sometimes *substantiated intuition, credentialed authority*, and *tested tradition*. Reasonable faith moves in the same direction indicated by the facts, though it's a commitment or step that takes you further than the evidence alone can carry you.[3]

Coming back to my example of the mountain bike, I go out to ride when it seems safe, the bicycle is in good repair, the weather looks good, and the trail is inviting. I think I'll come back in one piece, but it still takes some faith (although only a little) to get on the bike. This faith is *action* based on *good evidence*.

Likewise, I believe in aviation. I accept what I understand about the science of flight. But just acknowledging those facts didn't get me from Orange County to Kansas City earlier this week. I had to move beyond *agreeing* with the information and actually *exercise enough faith* (a moderate amount) to climb on board the airplane and fly to Missouri.

I honor the idea of marriage. I think the singular commitment of a man and a woman to one another for life is good for them, for their offspring, and for society in general. But that belief alone doesn't make me a husband. I still had to court the girl, pop the question, stand in front of the church, and say "I do." (That one took lots of faith—on *Heidi's* part!) And I still have to get up every morning and live out that commitment every day.

I had to move beyond agreeing *with the* information and actually *exercise* enough faith *(a moderate amount)* to climb on board *the airplane.*

In each of these examples, faith entails two components: *right belief* (the bike is sound, the airplane will fly, the girl and I were made for each other) and *appropriate action* (I'll ride that bike, fly in that airplane, marry that girl). But how do those components—right belief and appropriate action—apply to the task of choosing your faith?

Well, you can review the previous three chapters for my understanding of the right belief part. In them, I laid out twenty reasons for trusting not only in a powerful and wise deity, but in the God of Christianity. Many more arguments could be offered, but I'm confident that the ones I've given are solid and will point you toward truth. I hope I've at least convinced you of that—or that further research on your part will finish the job. For a quick review, here are the twenty reasons, or arrows, I identified:

Arrow 1 ⋯⟩ Design in the universe points to an *Intelligent Designer.*

Arrow 2 ⋯⟩ Fine tuning in the universe points to an intentional *Fine Tuner.*

Arrow 3 ⋯⟩ Information encoded into DNA points to a *Divine Encoder.*

Arrow 4 ⋯⟩ The beginning of the universe points to a *Divine Originator.*

Arrow 5 ⋯⟩ The sense of morality throughout the human race points to a *Moral Lawgiver.*

Arrow 6 ⋯⟩ The Bible shows itself to be a uniquely *consistent* religious book.

Arrow 7 ⋯⟩ The Bible is a uniquely *historical* religious book.

Arrow 8 ⋯⟩ The Bible is a uniquely *preserved* work of antiquity.

Arrow 9 ⋯⟩ Archaeology shows the Bible to be a powerfully *verified* book.

Arrow 10 ⋯⟩ The Bible shows itself to be a uniquely *honest* religious book.

Arrow 11 ⋯⟩ *Miracles*, performed in the presence of believers and critics alike, point to the prophets, apostles, and Jesus as messengers of God.

Arrow 12 ⋯⟩ *Fulfilled prophecies* point to the Bible as a divinely inspired book and to Jesus as the unique Messiah of God.

Arrow 13 ⋯⟩ Jesus' *sinless life* backed up his claim to be the Son of God.

Arrow 14 ⋯⟩ Jesus' *resurrection* powerfully established his credentials as the Son of God.

Arrow 15 ⋯⟩ The *emergence of the church* points to the authenticity of its message.

Arrow 16 ⋯⟩ The *changed lives of early skeptics* affirmed the truth of Jesus' resurrection and the teachings of the church.

Arrow 17 ⋯⟩ The *willingness of the disciples to die* for claims they knew to be true affirms the trustworthiness of their claims.

Arrow 18 ⋯⟩ The *changed minds of many modern skeptics* further support the Christian truth claims.

Arrow 19 ⋯⟩ The *testimonies of countless believers* throughout history attest to the reality of God and the value of following Jesus.

Arrow 20 ⋯⟩ It's true because *Jesus said so*—and he has the credentials to speak with authority.

∞

Before I move on from the *right belief* component of faith, let me explain why I've described these reasons as *arrows*: It's because each one points *toward* a truth or set of truths and *away* from all opposing viewpoints. Individually and collectively, they present ideas that take you in a particular direction.

Here's a picture portraying this with the arrows representing the various arguments:

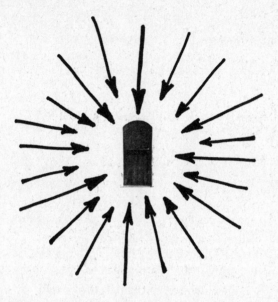

Now, as I mentioned before, many more reasons could be added (and thus, more arrows), though not every one will be equally compelling to every individual. But the cumulative case—what lawyers call the preponderance of evidence—presents an awfully powerful argument for the truth being in the center of that chart. I'm not claiming it is absolute proof; no faith choice ever is (including atheism, agnosticism, or whichever religion or sets of beliefs you currently adhere to). But from my study and observation, there is no other faith system that comes close to the kind of collective pattern of reasons and evidence we see in this diagram.

So, again, whatever the truth is, it seems clear that it must fall somewhere in the middle of the picture. And what, specifically, is in the middle? When you look at all of the reasons listed, it's clear they point to *belief in one God* who designed us and the universe, in *Jesus as God's human incarnation*, and in the Hebrew and Christian scriptures (Old and New Testaments) as *God's revelation*.

Anyone who wants to argue for a completely different position has a dual task at hand: (1) to refute the reasons pointing to the middle of the chart, and (2) to come up with other reasons that point compellingly in a different direction. For example, atheists need to do more than try to shoot down the arguments for God's existence; for their belief to rise above the level of a mere "leap of faith in the dark," they need to present arguments *for* the atheist position. The same goes for the Hindu, Buddhist, Baha'i, or New Age point of view—or any other.

But it's not enough just to know and agree with these conclusions about what's in the middle. Again, faith entails two components: right belief and *appropriate action based on that belief.* Knowing that the building is on fire doesn't save me from the smoke and heat. I must act on that knowledge and rush outside!

Likewise, I must do more than merely acknowledge the existence of the God of Christianity, nodding my head in agreement to a list of biblical teachings. I must also respond to that God and what he has said. It was Jesus who asked his listeners, "Why do you keep calling me 'Lord, Lord!' when you don't do what I say?"[4] Faith is both right belief *and* appropriate action—moving in the direction that the evidence points.

Just to be clear, that evidence, including what Jesus said and what he endorsed in the broader biblical writings, comprises God's central message: He loves us, but we each have disobeyed and dishonored him, thus breaking off our relationship with him. And we need his rescue and reclamation. That may be hard to hear, but there's an exciting upside: God chose to rescue us through Jesus, who came to earth not only to teach us and show us how to live but also to pay the penalty for our failure to live the way we should.

You see, our disobedience to God (what the Bible calls *sin*) resulted in a serious moral debt, a spiritual death penalty that each of us has earned but can never fully pay—in this life or the next. On our own, we are helpless to do anything about it.

But God doesn't want to leave us in this hopeless predicament. He cares too much about us not to provide us with a way of escape. So he came to earth in human flesh in the person of Jesus, and at the appointed time, he allowed Jesus to be accused, tried, and executed—not because he had done anything wrong, but because *we* had.

Jesus summed up his mission by saying that he came "not to be served but to serve others and to give his life as a ransom for many."[5] In effect, he came and willingly paid the death penalty in our place, on the cross, as a sort of "ransom payment" for you and for me.

∞

So what are we supposed to do with all this information? Two things: (1) study and reflect on it until we come to the point where we are able to grasp and, I trust, acknowledge its truth —including the reality of our need for God's rescue and reclamation; and (2) act on it by asking God to forgive our sins and to take control of our lives. Simple as it may seem, it's this act of humble repentance that God is patiently waiting for us to take. Or, to put it in a more familiar way, it's the kind of faith he's waiting for us to choose.

These two steps are so simple—and yet for some people they're so hard to do! Why is that? What are the barriers that can hold us back from believing and doing what appear to be the right things? Here are a dozen common obstacles to taking that step of faith:

1. *Lack of Information.* You can't will yourself into believing something you don't understand. If what I've presented seems interesting and perhaps even intriguing, but you feel as if there are too many gaps in your understanding or too many questions left unanswered, then it's important that you slow down and do whatever it takes to find the necessary information first. That might include going back over the twenty arrows and reflecting on the reasons presented there. But you might need to go deeper by studying some of the next-step books and resources I've listed on page 267.

God doesn't want to leave us in this hopeless predicament. He cares too much about us not to provide us with a way of escape.

Do what it takes to gain and grasp the basics, but don't set the standard overly high for how much you need to know. Jesus, who taught clearly and advocated a strong understanding, also said we need to come to him like children, with a simple, trusting faith.

Recently, my laser printer stopped functioning. I opened its front panel and stared blankly inside, slowly realizing that I had no idea why it had quit working. Then a deeper realization struck me: I also had no idea why it had ever *worked*. Likewise, I don't genuinely grasp how my computer works or even how the lightbulb in my desk lamp functions and helps me see. We're surrounded by tools and technology that we use every day, even though we don't fully *get* how they work.

Faith is much like that. We need to learn enough to make sure we're on the right track toward choosing the right faith, but we won't grasp the whole thing in depth—and we would

be wise *not* to delay our decision about what to believe until we do. It's like a courtroom situation: The jury must gather and grasp as much information as it can, but then it must reach a verdict based on limited information and within a limited time span.

We need to learn enough to make sure we're on the right track toward choosing the right faith, but we won't grasp the whole thing in depth.

One question to consider while you're deliberating about the Christian faith is this: How sure are you about your *current* faith? Remember, all the while that you're weighing the evidence and deciding about Christian beliefs, you're clinging to some other belief system. In other words, you're not neutral. Right now you're living according to some basic set of beliefs about spiritual realities and God (or the lack of God). So let me ask you: Do you have better evidence for your current beliefs than you now have for Christianity? If not, it might be time to consider a move.

2. *Lack of Openness.* This one is hard to admit—and often difficult to see in ourselves. For a variety of reasons, we tend to approach new information while still limited by old pre-

suppositions and prejudices. As liberal theologian Rudolf Bultmann stated famously in the early 1940s, "It is impossible to use electric light and the wireless and to avail ourselves of modern medical and surgical discoveries, and at the same time to believe in the New Testament world of spirits and miracles."[6] That kind of predetermination about what is possible or impossible will limit us from authentically considering the actual evidence, especially when it points to the "world of spirits and miracles." It's much better—and wiser—to open our minds and let the evidence lead us where it will. Along the way, we can figure out what really *might* be possible.

3. *Intellectual Doubt or Disagreement.* In response to my drawing of the twenty arrows of information on page 226, some people would offer a few "anti-arrows," or intellectual arguments that challenge and seemingly undermine the "preponderance of evidence" pointing to the middle of the chart. These anti-arrows would appear as arrows that point out from the center. The two most common objections I've seen people raise are the problem of evil and the issue of suffering. Entire books have been written on these topics, but let me offer a few thoughts that I think are relevant.

First, some people contend that the existence of evil means that there can't be a good, wise, and powerful God, like the one I've described, because he would want to put a stop to evil and would have the power to do so. The fact that evil has not been stopped, the argument goes, indicates that this kind of a good, wise, and powerful God does not exist.

The Bible teaches that the reason God has not yet stopped all evil (which would involve putting a stop to the ones doing the evil—namely, *humanity*) is because of his patience toward us.[7] But there's an even more fundamental question that must be asked: *What is evil* in the absence of a Moral Lawgiver? Apart from there being a Moral Lawgiver (as we discussed in chapter 9), there can be no objective standard of right and wrong, or good and evil. So, from an atheist's perspective, if you follow the reasoning all the way out, it all comes down to personal preferences or cultural norms. In other words, rape and murder may not be my cup of tea, but they could be yours. They might be distasteful and unseemly to me, but apart from a transcendent standard, I can't really say that they're *wrong*.

But there's a huge problem with this line of thinking: You and I *really do know* that rape and murder are wrong. And this universal sense points us once again to a universal Standard Bearer who has woven a sense of morality into our very nature.

So, even the fact of evil points to the reality of a good God. And the arrow that seemed to be pointing away from the center is actually pointing back in.

∞

What about suffering? This one is difficult to address, especially in this limited space. But here are four thoughts:

First, no answer, no rationale, no philosophy, and no quote from the Bible will make you feel good about the difficult things you're going through in your life. Sometimes we make a mistake by trying to answer a question rather than just extending what is most needed at the time: love, mercy, comfort, and companionship. So, if you're in pain or if you're suffering right now, I don't want to trivialize what you're enduring by offering what will inevitably feel like simplistic responses. Please feel free to skip down about seven paragraphs and come back to my thoughts about suffering at another time—and may God's peace and comfort be with you in the meantime.

Now, if you're still with me, it's worth pointing out that the kind of suffering we face in this life was predicted by Jesus. He warned us forthrightly that "here on earth you will have many trials and sorrows."[8] More broadly, Jesus and all the writers of the Bible describe a world where there is sin, conflict, betrayal, and war—much like what we see around us every day and learn about in the nightly news.

So, second, even though these hard things bring pain and loss, it's good to know that the faith system represented by Jesus is truthful in refusing to gloss over the harsh aspects of the world in which we live. Christianity doesn't try to convince us, as some religions do, that we're all basically good, sharing a common spark of divinity within our hearts, and living in an increasingly utopian world where evil is a mere illusion. In sharp contrast to that misguided, but popular, worldview, Jesus cautions us that there will be pain and suffering. Thankfully, he immediately added these words of encouragement: "But take heart, because I have overcome the world."[9]

Apart from there being a Moral Lawgiver, there can be no objective standard of right and wrong, or good and evil.

Third, Jesus didn't just warn us about suffering in this world; he personally experienced it in a measure greater than we can imagine. He cared for other people while lacking a home for himself. He faced resistance, ridicule, rejection, and scorn—and numerous attempts on his life—as he sought to teach and reach people just like you and me. And after three thankless years, he was finally betrayed by a friend, abandoned by his partners, falsely accused by the religious elite, tortured, and then killed in a brutal and shameful fashion between two common thieves. If anyone understands unjust suffering, and if anyone can offer us help and comfort in our times of need, it's Jesus, the Son of God, who endured such unthinkable things himself. He "understands our weaknesses, for he faced all of the same testings we do, yet he did not sin. So let us come boldly to the throne of our gracious God. There we will receive his mercy, and we will find grace to help us when we need it most."[10]

Finally, our experience of suffering points us logically back to God (in much the same way as the problem of evil). C. S. Lewis, in his earlier days as an atheist, used to ask, "If a good God made the world, why has it gone wrong?"[11] Here's the answer he later gave:

My argument against God was that the universe seemed so cruel and unjust. But how had I got this idea of *just* and *unjust*? A man does not call a line crooked unless he has some idea of a straight line. What was I comparing this universe with when I called it unjust? If the whole show was bad and senseless from A to Z, so to speak, why did I, who was supposed to be part of the show, find myself in such violent reaction against it? . . .

Thus in the very act of trying to prove that God did not exist—in other words, that the whole of reality was senseless— I found I was forced to assume that one part of reality—namely my idea of justice—was full of sense. Consequently, atheism turns out to be too simple. If the whole universe has no meaning, we should never have found out that it has no meaning: just as, if there were no light in the universe and therefore no creatures with eyes, we should never know it was dark. *Dark* would be without meaning.[12]

∞

Aside from the issues of pain and suffering, another common objection to Christianity is the apparent contradictions in the Bible (such as differences among the Gospels of Matthew, Mark, Luke, and John). For example, critics point to the fact that one Gospel account says there was an angel at the tomb on the first Easter morning, and another Gospel says there were *two* angels. "How can you trust the New Testament accounts about the Resurrection when the writers can't even keep track of how many angels there supposedly were at the empty tomb?"

Christianity doesn't try to convince us that we're all basically good, sharing a common spark of divinity within our hearts.

First, most of these so-called contradictions are not even serious problems. For example, if there were "two angels," then it's also accurate to say there was "an angel." Note that the second witness doesn't say "*only* one angel," which would have been a contradiction. If two reporters came and looked in my office right now, and if one of them later wrote, "Mark had a lamp on his desk," and the other mentioned in more detailed fashion that "Mark has two lamps on his desk," they would both be right. A third observer might add even more facts, saying, "The guy must really like light—he has three lamps in his office." All three accounts would be accurate.[13]

Critics seem to overlook the fact that slight differences in eyewitness accounts of any event are actually earmarks of their truthfulness. It's when every witness says the exact same thing, in the exact same way, that we should become suspicious. The diversity in the Gospel descriptions tells us that the writers did not conspire to "get their stories straight" in order to foist a fable on us about something they made up.

Critics seem to overlook the fact that slight differences in eyewitness accounts of any event are actually earmarks of their truthfulness.

There are some hard questions and some serious challenges to the Christian faith, but in my experience, the deeper I look, the more confident I become. And the wealth of books, articles, and Web sites that offer credible information and answers from highly credentialed scholars and teachers seems to increase by the day.

Here's my advice: Raise your doubts and questions, but do your research and homework. If this faith is built on real facts, as I've claimed, it will stand the test of scrutiny.

4. *Lack of Experience.* In our culture, people increasingly want more than just information and ideas; they're after a genuine *experience*. They don't just want coffee; they want a Starbucks experience. They don't just want a restaurant with good music; they want the Hard Rock Cafe. They don't just want a bookstore; they want a Barnes & Noble or Borders superstore, where they can have the coffee experience, listen to great music, sit in a nice leather chair, and peruse some good books.

It's similar in the spiritual realm—people don't just want information, the facts and figures; they want a genuine spiritual experience. It's great to know that churches and ministries are increasingly offering these kinds of opportunities in their public services, as well as in their smaller study groups and classes. These are safe places people can just visit, or they can become a regular part of the group. Once there, they can be real and not pretend to know what they don't know or to agree with what they don't agree with. And they can ask questions about things they're not sure about—even hard or challenging questions—and talk openly about them.

If you'll take the initiative to visit a church or group like I'm describing, I'm confident it will be a great boost in your journey of faith.[14]

5. *Lifestyle Issues.* This is another one of those personal issues that can be hard to detect, but how you are living can have a huge impact on what you're open to considering or embracing. If you perceive that choosing faith in Jesus will require you to let go of certain aspects of your lifestyle that you'd rather not release, then you might find yourself intuitively looking for excuses not to follow Jesus. It's like the story told about comedian W. C. Fields, who when asked why near the end of his life he was seen reading the Bible, replied, "I'm looking for loopholes, my friend. Looking for loopholes."

On a more serious note, Aldous Huxley, the well-known author and atheist, offered the following honest confession:

I had motives for not wanting the world to have a meaning; consequently assumed that it had none, and was able without any difficulty to find satisfying reasons for this assumption.... For myself, as, no doubt, for most of my contemporaries, the philosophy of meaninglessness was essentially an instrument of liberation. The liberation we desired was simultaneously liberation from a certain political and economic system and liberation from a certain system of morality. *We objected to the morality because it interfered with our sexual freedom.*[15]

As you consider the implications of choosing your faith, try to pull back the covers on what is influencing your decision or perhaps putting a drag on it. What would you need to give up or change? Often *that* is the issue much more than questions about the evidence for the miracles of Jesus or how many angels there were at his empty tomb.

Whatever the issue is, I'm confident that the surpassing benefits of knowing God and his forgiveness and leadership will outweigh what you might need to alter or give up. But that's a determination, and a decision, that you're going to have to make for yourself.

Perhaps you've said something like this: "If that's what Jesus and his people are like, then I don't want to have anything to do with him or his church."

6. *Personal Hurts.* Sometimes the below-the-surface impediment is not an intellectual question or a lifestyle issue, but it's a personal experience or hurt that makes it hard to consider moving in the direction of faith. Perhaps you were around someone who claimed to be a religious person but was a thorough-going hypocrite. Perhaps you've said something like this: "If that's what Jesus and his people are like, then I don't want to have anything to do with him or his church."

I've got news for you: that's *not* what Jesus is like. In fact, do you know who dislikes hypocrisy even more than you do? Jesus![16] So he's right there with you in how you feel about many of the inconsistencies and shortcomings of people who claim to represent him.

If your personal hurts are of a different nature, all I can say is that God is your best source of healing and wholeness. I don't say that because I know your pain or experience, because obviously I don't—but God knows, and I'm fully convinced that he cares. He made you, and he loves you. Jesus is the one who said, "Come to me, all of you who are weary and carry heavy burdens, and I will give you rest."[17]

Instead of resisting and running from God, move toward him, asking him for help and healing in the midst of your pain.

7. Sense of Control. Friedrich Nietzsche once declared boldly: "We deny God as God. . . . If the existence of this Christian God were *proved* to us, we should feel even less able to believe in him."[18] This is the same man who became famous for his philosophy that life is all about "the will to power." He also became infamous for his statement that "God is dead."[19]

Although Nietzsche took it to the extreme, his thoughts represent a struggle that many of us have had: We desire to stay in control, relinquishing none of our freedom or autonomy to any outside forces or higher powers—God included.

C. S. Lewis described the problem from a different angle, but in his characteristically accessible way:

> There is one vice of which no man in the world is free; which every one in the world loathes when he sees it in someone else; and of which hardly any people . . . ever imagine that they are guilty themselves. . . .
>
> The essential vice, the utmost evil, is *Pride*. Unchastity, anger, greed, drunkenness, and all that, are mere fleabites in

comparison: it was through Pride that the devil became the devil: Pride leads to every other vice: it is the complete anti-God state of mind. . . .

In God you come up against something which is in every respect immeasurably superior to yourself. Unless you know God as that—and, therefore, know yourself as nothing in comparison—you do not know God at all. As long as you are proud you cannot know God. A proud man is always looking down on things and people: and, of course, as long as you are looking down, you cannot see something that is above you.[20]

You might want to go back and read that passage again, maybe a couple of times; it is penetratingly true, and yet its meaning is persistently elusive. Pride is, as Lewis describes, so easy to see in others and yet so hard to detect in ourselves—and it's completely devastating when left unchecked and unchallenged. While all of the other sins make you wonder whether God can accept you, pride makes you foolishly wonder whether you'll accept God.

8. *Anger.* This one might surprise you, as it did me when a friend of mine recently admitted how he'd struggled with anger during his own spiritual search. "Why anger?" I asked him. He explained that the implications of the claims of Christ are so stark and so challenging, especially if you're a member of another religion as he had been before becoming a follower of Jesus, that sometimes you just don't know how to deal with them. "So you're telling me that my parents are wrong, my religion is wrong—including our prophet and holy books, and that even the collective culture I grew up in is wrong," my friend said by way of example, in order to help me better understand. "I just don't want to hear about it!"

Is anger clouding up the issues for you as well? If so, try to let it go. It might help to start by acknowledging that, yes, your parents, religion, and society might actually be wrong, at least in part. And you're not going to know until you carefully check it out. That was a central thrust of Jesus' ministry as he lovingly but courageously sought to correct elements in his own culture and helped people move toward what was right.

If what you've been taught really is misguided, getting angry about it isn't going to change that fact one way or the other— or help anybody. Try to move past this normal and natural knee-jerk reaction and pursue the truth that Jesus promised "will set you free."[21]

9. *Discomfort.* This one is simple to grasp; Change can be hard. It's always easier to stick with the *status quo* and put off new things for a new day—a day that may never come. But it's actually much better to face discomfort now as you confront the questions and search for truth, rather than have to deal later

If what you've been taught really is misguided, getting angry about it isn't going to change that fact one way or the other.

with the distraught feelings of knowing you saw the better way but wasted time, or even lost the opportunity completely, by doing what at the time seemed like playing it safe.

10. *Disinterest.* This is one of the hardest obstacles to deal with because old-fashioned apathy, by definition, doesn't care enough to bother with issues of truth and faith. We now live in a secular society that seems to make a studied effort to ignore or neglect true spirituality. Call it the national religion of passive and pervasive *"whateverism."*

But here's some good news: The fact that you've read this far into a book about spiritual truth is a good sign that you have not yet succumbed to rampant disinterest and apathy. Let me urge you to take whatever level of interest you have and expand on it. Fan it into a flame. Make your spiritual pursuit a front-burner issue. As Jesus described, seek after the "pearl of great value."[22]

In the meantime, don't forget that you're not in a neutral position. Right now, you are staking your life on whatever spiritual perspective you're currently trusting in.

11. *Fear.* Sometimes resistance or hesitation goes undefined—but they can stem from an underlying fear that is very real. This can be from a natural discomfort with the unknown, as mentioned above, or it can have a more sinister source. This may be a new thought to you, but according to Jesus and the message of the Bible, there is an ongoing but unseen spiritual battle raging in our minds. Jesus wasn't kidding when he said that Satan is like a thief who "comes only to steal and kill and destroy."[23]

I realize this may seem far-fetched. And the whole thing might be easy to write off, were it not for those inaudible, but very real, internal whisperings:

- Don't get too serious about these matters of faith.

- Today would not be a good day to choose.

- You've got too much to do before letting go of your freedom and putting on a religious straightjacket.

- You're really above all this and don't need it.

- You don't know enough—or you may actually know too much, including how far you've fallen and how unworthy and beyond the reach of grace and redemption you really are.

- It's too late for someone like you, and there's really nothing you can do about it, except find ways to distract yourself and escape or to medicate yourself and numb the pain.

I'm guessing that some of these conflicting and personally defeating messages are not new to you. As C. S. Lewis colorfully illustrates in his insightful little book *The Screwtape Letters*, the devil is cunning and clever and untiring in his efforts to sabotage our spiritual progress. But in our "enlightened" society, belief in the existence of an actual devil is not really in vogue. The late Keith Green, a Christian musician who died in a plane crash in 1982, captured the mood of our society in winsome fashion when he sang a song from the perspective of Satan—"No One Believes in Me Anymore":

OH, MY JOB KEEPS GETTING EASIER

AS TIME KEEPS SLIPPING AWAY

I CAN IMITATE YOUR BRIGHTEST LIGHT

AND MAKE YOUR NIGHT LOOK JUST LIKE DAY

I PUT SOME TRUTH IN EVERY LIE

TO TICKLE ITCHING EARS

YOU KNOW I'M DRAWING PEOPLE JUST LIKE FLIES

'CAUSE THEY LIKE WHAT THEY HEAR

I'M GAINING POWER BY THE HOUR

THEY'RE FALLING BY THE SCORE

YOU KNOW, IT'S GETTING VERY SIMPLE NOW

'CAUSE NO ONE BELIEVES IN ME ANYMORE.[24]

It's time we started believing—and fighting back. The apostle James tells us how:

> So humble yourselves before God. *Resist the devil, and he will flee from you. Come close to God, and God will come close to you.* Wash your hands, you sinners; purify your hearts, for your loyalty is divided between God and the world. Let there be tears for what you have done. Let there be sorrow and deep grief. Let there be sadness instead of laughter, and gloom instead of joy. Humble yourselves before the Lord, and he will lift you up in honor.[25]

Thankfully, in the same conversation where Jesus warns us about the devil's plan to "steal and kill and destroy," he also says, "I am the gate. Those who come in through me will be saved. . . . My purpose is to give them a rich and satisfying life."[26]

Down through the ages, countless religious systems have been devised— some quite elaborate— to try to provide ways for us to earn our way back to God.

12. *Oversimplicity.* Okay, I invented that word, but I think it describes a real problem, which is the normal human reaction to the simple message of God's grace. We tell ourselves, "He can't just send Jesus to die on the cross and pay the penalty in my place. Trusting in Jesus might be good, but that can't be enough. Somehow I've got to figure out a way to pay him back!"

And so, down through the ages, countless religious systems have been devised—some quite elaborate—to try to provide ways for us to earn our way back to God. Though he is unimaginably holy, we attempt to appease him and to earn our way into his good favor. What's really confusing is that some of these payback schemes are constructed under the banner of Christianity. But they confound and confuse the uncomplicated message of grace and redemption that is freely available by choosing faith in Jesus Christ.

Against this human tendency to make things more complicated than they are, I'll say it again: We need to let Jesus speak for himself. He's the one who simply and straightforwardly summed it all up with these famous words:

> For God loved the world so much that he gave his one and
> only Son, so that everyone who believes in him will not perish
> but have eternal life. God sent his Son into the world not to
> judge the world, but to save the world through him. There is no
> judgment against anyone who believes in him.[27]

What does it mean to *believe* in Jesus? It includes believing what he taught about himself: He is God incarnate who came to earth to "seek and save those who are lost"—*namely us.*[28] But more than just embracing a set of ideas, we need to receive the *person* who said he is the truth.[29] Jesus wants to be not only our forgiver, but also our leader and friend. And it all starts when we call on the name of the Lord, for "everyone who calls on the name of the LORD will be saved."[30]

So, let me urge you one more time: Be a lover of truth. Seek it—and Jesus, who is the truth—with everything you've got, because he promised that if you'll seek, you will find.

CHAPTER THIRTEEN

THE *BENEFITS* OF CHOOSING YOUR FAITH WISELY

I'M WOVEN IN A FANTASY, I CAN'T BELIEVE THE
    THINGS I SEE
THE PATH THAT I HAVE CHOSEN NOW HAS LED ME
    TO A WALL
AND WITH EACH PASSING DAY I FEEL A LITTLE MORE
    LIKE SOMETHING DEAR WAS LOST
IT RISES NOW BEFORE ME, A DARK AND SILENT
    BARRIER BETWEEN,
ALL I AM, AND ALL THAT I WOULD EVER WANT TO BE . . .

Kerry Livgren, "The Wall"[1]

My father's words were freeing and frightening to me—at the same time.

I was nearing the end of my eighteenth year, living in my parents' home, working full-time at a stereo store, and trying to figure out whether I should go to college or do something else with my life. From a faith standpoint, I had been out on a spiritual excursion for several years, still believing what I'd been taught growing up, but not living it very well.

In order to make it to the safety of my bedroom, I had to get to a short staircase that led to the upper floor of the house. This meant walking past the area near the fireplace where my dad would often sit at night reading his newspaper. There was no other way to get upstairs, except by climbing through a second-story window (which I'd already tried a couple of times—it was too much work). I loved my parents, but during that era of my life, I'd try to avoid getting caught in a conversation that might become a bit too personal for my comfort level.

One particular evening, I tried to slip surreptitiously past the danger zone to the sanctuary of my room. But unfortunately, with my father's sharp eye and keen sense of timing, I was caught.

"Mark," my dad said in a gentle but abrupt voice that stopped me in my tracks. He looked up from the paper and asked, "Do you have a minute?"

"Sure," I said, trying to sound as casual as possible. "What's up?"

"I've been wanting to talk to you about something," he replied. Confident that this couldn't be good, I asked him what it was about. "You're reaching the age, son, when you're making important, life-changing decisions. And as your mom and

I have been talking and praying about that, we've reached a conclusion I wanted to share with you."

Knowing he probably wasn't ramping up to tell me they had decided to divvy out the inheritance funds early, I hesitantly replied, "Okay, what is it?"

"We wanted to tell you that we've done our best to raise you in the nurture and admonition of the Lord." (That's old-fashioned King James Bible language from Ephesians 6:4. It means to teach your child how to follow and please God.) "We've done about all we can do to teach and point you in the right direction in your faith, but you're already, what, eighteen years old?"

"Yep, almost nineteen," I replied.

"Well, you're a young man now, and you are at the age where you'll have to start deciding for yourself what you believe and how you're going to live your life. Our job as parents is pretty much finished. We can't make up your mind for you, and we don't want to try to force you to do or be anything you really don't want to."

Okay, I thought. *So far, so good.*

"So," he continued, saying those freeing but frightening words I alluded to at the beginning of the chapter, "we want you to know that we're now giving you over to the Lord and putting you in his hands. We'll always be here to help and encourage in any way we can—and you know we want you to follow Jesus—but what you decide and do from here on out will ultimately be between you and God."

"Okay," I said, not quite sure how to react. "Thanks for letting me know." Then I turned and walked up to my room, feeling a sense of relief that perhaps the pressure would finally be off for going to church every Sunday, pretending to be religious, and so forth. But as I weighed what he'd said, the "giving you over to the Lord, and putting you in his hands" part was a bit scary. I mean, I could avoid—or trick—my *parents*, at least part of the time. But *God*? Wasn't he supposed to be everywhere, seeing everything we do and knowing every thought we think? That made me feel really uncomfortable.

∞

Reflecting back now, years later, I can see that my parents were really wise in how they handled me. They steered me toward truth my entire life, but when adulthood came, they let me choose my own faith.

I can see that my parents were really wise in how they handled me. They steered me toward truth my entire life, but they let me choose my own faith.

A few weeks after that pivotal discussion with my dad—when, at age nineteen, I finally got sick of playing religious games while living a hypocritical life—I finally made my decision. It was not a momentous event—at least not on the surface; it was really more of a quiet affirmation of what I knew to be true and a choice to finally respond and act on that knowledge.

It was late in the evening. I was driving my car on the outskirts of my hometown. The prayer itself was simple, and I kept my eyes open while I prayed (I was, after all, driving at the time). I don't remember whether I said the words out loud or just expressed them in my mind, but I guess it doesn't make any difference to God, who knows our thoughts. Basically, all I said was, "Dear God, I'm tired of pretending, going my own way, making a mess of my life, and wasting so much time. I need and ask you to forgive my sins and to take control of my life. Please accept me as your son, and I'll do my best to follow you from here on out—from now until eternity. In Jesus' name, amen."

Brilliant bursts of fireworks? Nope. Miraculous signs, shooting stars, angels with special messages suddenly sitting in the backseat? None of that. Just a sense of God's presence and pleasure, a changed heart, a feeling of joy and relief, and the confidence that I was now beginning a truly revolutionized life. And it has been an adventure ever since. It's ironic, but my greatest fear in surrendering control of my life to Jesus was that I would lose that sense of fun and excitement—and it's been exactly the opposite.

My greatest fear in surrendering control of my life to Jesus was that I would lose that sense of fun and excitement—and it's been exactly the opposite.

Yes, there are ups and downs, and every day is not necessarily better than the day before. But God has opened doors to serving and making a difference in the lives of others; to finding my purpose, and in some measure fulfilling it; to moving through life with a sense of confidence that God is with me, that my life matters, and that I can make a real impact in this world; and to enjoying the assurance that I'm forgiven and don't have to live in fear, regret, shame, or apprehension. On top of that, I know that someday I'm going to die, and then things will get even *better*.

∞

Thinking through some of the themes of this book, it's reassuring to know that I've embraced truth that's real—that genuinely reflects *what is*—and I don't need to manufacture my own relativistic or pragmatic versions of wishful thinking and then live my life hoping against hope that they will turn out to be right.

It was when I quit clinging to traditional ideas that I ended up confirming much of the content and reason behind the traditions I had been taught. Today I can enjoy those traditions and pass many of them on to my kids, not as mindless habits or family obligations, but as tested practices that remind us of actual truth and reality.

I have an authority in my life that has not been imposed on me, but that I've willingly accepted and embraced because it—that is, *he*—has credentials like no other. And the revelation he has provided, namely the Bible, also has established itself again and again as a trustworthy source of inspiration, spiritual information, and guidance.

Today, I actually have more confidence in my intuitive instincts than I previously had because I can sense that those instincts have been trained and tutored by God's wisdom, and they are actively balanced by the occasional quiet but real mystical leadings of the Holy Spirit. These come sometimes as simple impulses that draw my attention to a certain need or opportunity. At other times, they are much more distinct impressions of God's presence or guidance.

Compared to some followers of Jesus, I feel as if I'm a fledgling when it comes to experiencing and following God's supernatural leadings. But there are times when God's presence is very evident and real to me. And there have been a few moments in my life when his touch has been almost overwhelming—such as the time I was sitting alone in a worship service in a church in London and the Holy Spirit enveloped me with emotion, tenderness, and a sense of his loving presence (actually, those words don't do it justice—but they're the best I can find to talk about it).

And there's no question—to me or anyone who knew me way back when—that God has blessed me with logic and reason that goes well beyond what I had as an average high school student prior to my choosing to follow him. The wielding of these instruments for the testing and trying of truth has given me a confidence that Christianity is not a blind trust or a mere leap of faith. It is a belief based on reliable data, history, and facts, as well as authentic experience. It's not just helpful; it's right and true.

The testing and trying of truth has given me a confidence that Christianity is not a blind trust or a mere leap of faith.

It is hard for me not to sound like some kind of PR agent or advertisement, but really knowing, following, and serving Jesus has been an incredibly exciting walk of faith—one I've never regretted and that I'm confident will never end. And it's from that perspective, as one not just convinced of truth but also experiencing an exhilarating relationship with the Creator, that I encourage you—no, *strongly urge* you—to consider choosing your faith as I did.

It's so easy in the rush and busyness of everyday life to view spiritual matters as esoteric or surreal—the stuff of saints and ascetics but not of ordinary people like you and me. But there will come a day, and we're all approaching it sooner than we probably think we are, when we'll be forced to face reality in the realm of faith and spirituality.

With surprising candor, Steve Jobs of Apple Computer, a man not known for metaphysical musings, said this to Stanford's 2005 graduating class:

> Remembering that I'll be dead soon is the most important tool
> I've ever encountered to help me make the big choices in life.
> Because almost everything—all external expectations, all pride,
> all fear of embarrassment or failure—these things just fall away
> in the face of death, leaving only what is truly important.[2]

I couldn't agree more. I would add only this: When considering matters of faith, why wait until we're close to death, hoping that we'll have the chance to "make our peace" and patch things up at the very end—when it's too late to discover the adventure or to live out the truth that we might finally find?

It doesn't make sense to wait, which is why my challenge to you is to consider and act upon these things *now*, so you can enjoy the benefits throughout the rest of your life here on earth, as well as later, into the next life.

∞

In a moment, you will be finished reading this book, and you'll close its cover—perhaps for the final time. As you do, take a few moments to look at the picture of the door on the front of the book, and to consider the decision it represents for you to choose your faith wisely. You might also want to meditate on what these words could mean for you: "Look! I stand at the door and knock. If you hear my voice and open the door, I will come in, and we will share a meal together as friends."[3]

NOTES

Chapter 1—"Why Choose *Any* Faith?"

1. This is from an interview with Michael Stipe of the band R.E.M. on BBC Radio 2. See the article and the link to the audio interview at www.bbc.co.uk/radio2/soldonsong/songlibrary/losingmyreligion.shtml.

2. "Losing My Religion" by William T. Berry, Peter Lawrence Buck, Michael E. Mills, and Michael Stipe. Copyright © 1991 Night Garden Music/Warner-Tamerlane Publishing Corp. (BMI). All rights reserved.

3. Frank Newport, "Americans More Likely to Believe in God than the Devil, Heaven More than Hell," *Gallup News Service*, June 13, 2007.

4. See Robert D. Putnum, *Bowling Alone: The Collapse and Revival of American Community* (Simon & Schuster, 2000), 97–98.

5. David Van Biema, "God vs. Science," *Time*, November 5, 2006.

6. To help you identify your current faith path, a self-assessment quiz is available in the booklet *Your Faith Path* by Mark Mittelberg (Tyndale, 2008).

Chapter 2—"This Is *My* Truth—You Find Your Own"

1. Transcribed and excerpted from a video of this exchange between Bill O'Reilly and Richard Dawkins on the Fox News television program *The O'Reilly Factor* on April 23, 2007, posted at www.youtube.com/watch?v=wECRvNRquvl.

2. John 18:38

3. Ronald Harwood, screenwriter for *The Pianist* (in "Story of Survival" in the DVD's bonus materials, starting at 7:20), Limited Soundrack Edition, 2003.

4. *A Companion to Epistemology (Blackwell Companions to Philosophy)* s.v. "Relativism."

5. Zechariah 8:19 says, "So love truth and peace."

6. *Oxford Companion to Philosophy*, s.v. "Socrates."

Chapter 3—"But I've *Always* Believed What I Believe"

1. Shirley Jackson, "The Lottery," *New Yorker*. June 28, 1948. Emphasis added.

2. Lee Strobel, *The Case for the Real Jesus* (Grand Rapids, MI: Zondervan, 2007), 249–250.

3. Mark 7:5-8. This passage is paralleled in Matthew 15:1-9. Occasionally throughout this book, I'll quote passages from the Bible. I'll give reasons in a later chapter for why I'm convinced the Bible has unique credentials that give strong evidence of its truthfulness and divine inspiration. But regardless of what you think of the Bible, I hope you'll seriously think about my reasons for quoting it here, and at least view these passages as ancient wisdom and history worthy of your consideration.

4. Isaiah 29:13

5. To read Lee Strobel's story of moving from atheism to faith, along with many of the discoveries that changed his mind, see his powerful book, *The Case for Christ* (Zondervan, 1998).

6. Matthew 7:7-8

7. Revelation 21:5

Chapter 4—"You'd *Better* Believe It!"

1. David Johnson and Jeff VanVonderen, *The Subtle Power of Spiritual Abuse: Recognizing and Escaping Spiritual Manipulation and False Spiritual Authority Within the Church* (Minneapolis, MN: Bethany House, 2005).

2. Thomas S. Kuhn, *The Structure of Scientific Revolutions* (Chicago: University of Chicago Press, 1996).

3. John Cougar Mellencamp, "The Authority Song."

4. 1 Thessalonians 5:21-22

5. Matthew 7:15-17

6. John 8:46

7. Mark 9:23-24

8. 1 Timothy 4:16

9. Jesus, in John 3:12. Norman Geisler and Ron Brooks comment about this verse in their book *When Skeptics Ask* (Baker, 1996): "Jesus expected His accuracy in factually testable matters to be proof that He was telling the truth about spiritual matters that cannot be tested" (148).

10. See Bill McKeever , "DNA and the Book of Mormon Record," online at http://www.mrm.org/topics/book-mormon/dna-and-book-mormon-record.

11. Deuteronomy 18:21-22

12. Robert and Gretchen Passantino, *Answers to the Cultist at Your Door* (Eugene, OR: Harvest House, 1981), 50–53.

13. 1 Thessalonians 1:5; Philippians 4:9

14. Nabeel Qureshi, "Crossing Over: An Intellectual and Spiritual Journey from Islam to Christianity," online at http://www.answering-islam.org/Authors/Qureshi/testimony.htm.

Chapter 5—"I Just *Feel* That It's True"

1. *Star Wars Episode IV: A New Hope*, directed by George Lucas (1977).

2. Bill Moyers, "Of Myth and Men," *Time*, April 18 1999.

3. "The TM Technique: Life in Accord with Natural Law," 1978. Online video at http://www.tm.org/video/index.html.

4. L. T. Jeyachandran, "Tough Questions about Hinduism and Transcendental Meditation," in *Who Made God?* ed. Ravi Zacharias and Norman Geisler (Grand Rapids, MI: Zondervan, 2003), 163–164.

5. Napoleon Hill, *Think and Grow Rich* (San Diego: Aventine, 2004), 221. Originally published by the Ralston Foundation, Meriden, CT, 1938.

6. Ibid., 234, 236.

7. Rhonda Byrne, *The Secret* (New York: Atria, 2006), 56.

8. Malcolm Gladwell, *Blink: The Power of Thinking Without Thinking* (New York: Little, Brown, 2005), 3.

9. Ibid., 4.

10. Ibid., 5.

11. Ibid., 5–6.

12. Ibid., 6.

13. Ibid., 7.

14. Ibid., 8.

15. Psalm 139:14, NIV

16. 2 Corinthians 2:13

17. Blaise Pascal, *Pensées* (New York: Penguin, 1995), 127.

18. L. T. Jeyachandran, "Tough Questions about Hinduism and Transcendental Meditation," in *Who Made God?* ed. Ravi Zacharias and Norman Geisler (Grand Rapids, MI: Zondervan, 2003), 164.

19. Gladwell, *Blink*, 14–15.

20. Proverbs 14:12

21. Jeremiah 17:9

22. John 10:27

Chapter 6—"God *Told* Me It's True!"

1. This conversation took place during a dialogue between Mormons and Evangelical Christians at Mariners Church in Irvine, California, Spring 2007.

2. See Revelation chapter 11.

3. Robert L. Millet, *Getting at the Truth: Responding to Difficult Questions about LDS Beliefs* (Salt Lake City: Deseret, 2004), 36.

4. Ibid.

5. Ibid., 37. (Millet is quoting Ezra Taft Benson [president of the Church of Jesus Christ of Latter-Day Saints from 1985–1994] in *A Witness and a Warning: A Modern-Day Prophet Testifies of the Book of Mormon* (Deseret, 1988), 13, 31.)

6. Ibid., 37–38. (Millet is quoting Gordon B. Hinckley [president of the Church of Jesus Christ of Latter-Day Saints since 1995] in *Faith, the Essence of True Religion* (Deseret, 1989), 10–11.)

7. Ibid., 38. (Millet is quoting Boyd K. Packer, "Conference Report," October 1985, 104, 107.)

8. Ibid., 39.

9. Ibid., 41.

10. See, for example, 3 Nephi, chapters 12–14, which is almost identical to the Sermon on the Mount in Matthew 5–7 of the King James Version of the Bible, including the additions in the KJV made for clarification and put in italics by the English translators. This is interesting in light of the fact that the original *Book of Mormon* purportedly was written more than a millennium before the King James Bible was produced in 1611.

11. These spiritual forces are referred to in Bible passages such 2 Corinthians 11:14 and Galatians 1:8-9.

12. 1 Thessalonians 5:21-22

13. 1 Thessalonians 5:19-20

14. For more information on Mormon teaching, see Bill McKeever and Eric Johnson, *Mormonism 101: Examining the Religion of the Latter-Day Saints* (Grand Rapids: Baker, 2000).

15. For further reading on the topic of Islam and Jesus, see Norman Geisler and Abdul Saleeb, *Answering Islam* (Baker, 2002).

16. For details of Joseph Smith's contradictory accounts of his original vision, see Lane Thuet, "Which First Vision Account Should We Believe?" (Mormonism Research Ministry), online at www.mrm.org/topics/historical-issues/which-first-vision-account-should-we-believe.

17. For many of the details on these "new revelations" and other issues, see Dr. Walter Martin, *The Maze of Mormonism* (Vision House, 1987).

18. A powerful book to read about the internal struggles and inconsistencies within the Watchtower Bible and Tract Society (the Jehovah's Witness organization) is Raymond Franz, *Crisis of Conscience: The Struggle between Loyalty to God and Loyalty to One's Religion* (Commentary Press, 2002). Franz is a former member of the governing body of the Jehovah's Witnesses.

19. Acts 17:11

20. Galatians 1:8-9, NIV

21. I'm not denying the importance of praying and asking God for guidance as we assess truth claims and figure out what to believe. But this is not to be done in a vacuum, ignoring what we already know. And we should never pray and ask God whether something is true or okay if he has already made it clear that it is not.

22. Matthew 4:5-7

23. Bill McKeever, "As God Is, Man May Become?" (Mormonism Research Ministry) online at www.mrm.org/topics/salvation/god-man-may-become.

24. Robert L. Millet, *Getting at the Truth: Responding to Difficult Questions about LDS Beliefs* (Salt Lake City: Deseret, 2004), 65. Note that the *Book of Moses* and *Doctrine and Covenants (D&C)* are part of the standard works of the Mormon faith.

25. Isaiah 43:10, 12-13

26. Isaiah 45:21-22

27. Malachi 3:6

28. I realize that some Mormon teachers try to make the claim that they are not polytheistic because although they believe in many gods, they only worship one. But some Hindus similarly believe in many gods yet focus their worship on only one, such as Brahma, Vishnu, Shiva, or even Kali—but that focus doesn't make them any less polytheistic.

29. Galatians 1:8, NIV. Emphasis added.

30. 2 Corinthians 11:14-15

31. 1 John 4:1, NIV

32. For one of many examples, see Deuteronomy 18:9-13.

33. Acts 9: 1-9, 17-19

34. St. Augustine, *The Confessions of St. Augustine*, condensed version online at www.christianbooksummaries.com.

35. Pascal never spoke of that night. The only way we know about it is that he had sewn the parchment with his account into his jacket, and it was discovered after his death. This was later included in a compilation of his teachings, based on fragments of his writings, and called Pascal's *Pensées*.

36. 1 Thessalonians 5:21-22

Chapter 7—"I've Gotta *See It* to Believe It"

1. These traditional Zen *koans* can be found online at www.terebess. hu/english/zen.html.

2. This "enlightening" explanation can be found online at http://thezenfrog. wordpress.com/2007/05/08/a-collection-of-zen-koans-and-stories-from-the-compilation-101-zen-stories. Scroll down to the end of "*The Sound of One Hand.*"

3. Norman L. Geisler and Frank Turek, *I Don't Have Enough Faith to Be an Atheist* (Wheaton, IL: Crossway, 2004), 54–55.

4. William Lane Craig, *Reasonable Faith*, rev. ed. (Wheaton, IL: Crossway Books, 1994), 40.

5. Patrick Zukeran, "Archaeology and the Old Testament," (Probe Ministries). The text of this article can be found online at www.probe.org.

6. Norman L. Geisler, *Baker Encyclopedia of Christian Apologetics* (Grand Rapids, MI: Baker, 1999), 702.

7. Ibid.

8. Ibid., 429. Emphasis added.

9. Stephen C. Meyer, "The Scientific Status of Intelligent Design," in *Science and Evidence for Design in the Universe* (San Francisco: Ignatius, 2000), 152–153.

10. Richard Dawkins, *The Blind Watchmaker* (New York: Norton, 1986), 1.

11. Ibid., 21.

12. Ibid., 36.

13. Ibid., 43.

14. Ibid., 5.

15. Richard Dawkins, *The God Delusion* (New York: Houghton Mifflin, 2006), 158. Emphasis added.

16. Marilynne Robinson, "Hysterical Scientism: The Ecstasy of Richard Dawkins," *Harper's* (November 2006).

17. Antony Flew and Roy Abraham Varghese, *There Is a God: How the World's Most Notorious Atheist Changed His Mind* (New York: HarperCollins, 2007), xiv-xv.

18. Ibid., xvi–xviii.

19. Associated Press, "Famous Atheist Now Believes in God," December 9, 2004.

20. Lee Strobel, "Why Top Atheist Now Believes in a Creator," November 2, 2006. Article can be found online at www.leestrobel.com.

Chapter 8—"I'm Thinking about How I *Think*—and *Choose*"

1. Todd Agnew, "Prelude," copyright © 2006 Ardent/Koala Music (ASCAP). All rights reserved. Used by permission.

2. Tom Neven, "Choosing Their Religion," *Plugged In*, August 2005. The article may be found online at http://go.family.org/davinci/content/A000000046.cfm.

3. BBC News, "Monarch faith role 'should stay,'" September 15, 2007. The article may be found online at http://news.bbc.co.uk/2/hi/uk_news/6996112.stm.

4. Tom Neven, "Choosing Their Religion."

5. Deborah Caldwell , "Goldie: Buddhist, Jew, Jesus Freak," online interview may be found at www.beliefnet.com/story/172/story_17266_2.html.

6. Matthew 7:7

7. John 8:32

8. 1 Thessalonians 5:21

9. 1 John 4:1

10. This conclusion is backed up in my understanding of the writings of numerous Christian philosophers and teachers, including John Warwick Montgomery, Norman Geisler, R. C. Sproul, E. J. Carnell, William Lane Craig, and Stuart C. Hackett.

11. This quote is one Bob often told me and others, but it was put in print, along with his overall story, by Gretchen Passantino-Coburn, Bob's wife and ministry partner for many years. The full story can be found online at www.answers.org/news/article.php?story=20071004173254274.

12. I recently contributed to a book written in honor of Bob and Gretchen Passantino, along with a number of other authors and teachers whose lives were affected by them. The book was edited by Norman Geisler and Chad V. Meister and is called *Reasons for Faith: Making a Case for the Christian Faith* (Crossway, 2007). Bob's wife and ministry partner of many years, Gretchen Passantino-Coburn, continues to lead their ministry, called Answers In Action (www.answers.org).

Chapter 9—"How Can I *Figure Out* What to Believe?"

1. "The Logical Song," words and music by Rick Davies and Roger Hodgson. Copyright © 1979 Almo Music Corporation/Delicate Music/Universal Music Publishing Group. All rights reserved.

2. Michael Denton, *Evolution: A Theory in Crisis* (Bethesda, MD: Adler & Adler, 1986), 328, 342.

3. Psalm 19:1

4. Romans 1:20

5. Richard Dawkins, *The God Delusion* (New York: Houghton Mifflin, 2006), 158.

6. "Star Survey Reaches 70 Sextillion," CNN.com, July 23, 2003. Available online at: www.cnn.com/2003/TECH/space/07/22/stars.survey.

7. Hugh Ross, *The Creator and the Cosmos* (Colorado Springs: NavPress, 1993), 111–114.

8. Lee Strobel, *The Case for a Creator* (Grand Rapids: Zondervan, 2004). This is the subtitle of chapter 6, pages 130–131. The quote of Fred Hoyle is from "The Universe: Past and Present Reflections," *Engineering & Science*, November 1981.

9. Ibid., 133–134.

10. Patrick Glynn, *God: The Evidence* (Roseville, CA: Prima, 1999), 53, 54–55.

11. Francis S. Collins, *The Language of God: A Scientist Presents Evidence for Belief* (New York: Free Press, 2006), 1–2.

12. Ibid., 2.

13. Ibid., 1, 3.

14. Lee Strobel, *The Case for a Creator* (Grand Rapids: Zondervan, 2004), 71.

15. From *Unlocking the Mystery of Life*, a DVD produced by Illustra Media. See www.illustramedia.com.

16. There are several versions of the cosmological argument. This one is called the kalam version, which is presented and defended in detail by many contemporary thinkers, especially William Lane Craig in his scholarly book *The Kalam Cosmological Argument* (Wipf & Stock, 1979). Craig also discusses it with Lee Strobel in *The Case for a Creator*, and Chad Meister offers a strong, straightforward explanation of it in his excellent book, *Building Belief* (Baker Books, 2006).

17. Albert Einstein, *Ideas and Opinions*, 1994 Modern Library Edition, copyright 1954 by Crown Publishers, Inc., published in the United States by Random House (New York), 43.

18. To use this point to try to argue that God must also have had a beginning is to misunderstand the meaning of *God*. He is eternal and did not have a beginning—and therefore does not have or need a cause. Unlike the universe and everything that is part of it, God is the cause behind the whole chain of effects and the only being sufficient to have produced such amazing effects, as we'll see.

19. Robert Jastrow, *God and the Astronomers*, 2nd ed. (New York: W.W. Norton, 1992), 103.

20. Ibid., 13.

21. Stephen Hawking and Roger Penrose, *The Nature of Space and Time* (Princeton, NJ: Princeton University Press, 2000), 20.

22. Genesis 1:1

23. Jastrow, *God and the Astronomers*, 107.

24. C. S. Lewis, *Mere Christianity*, (New York: HarperOne, 2001), 6–7.

25. Romans 2:15

26. Lee Strobel, *The Case for Faith* (Grand Rapids, MI: Zondervan, 2002), 250–251.

Chapter 10—"How Can I *Figure Out* What to Believe?"

1. Even though Jesus wasn't born until the time period covered in the New Testament, and is therefore never mentioned by name in the Old Testament, he is predicted and discussed—as the coming Messiah—many places in the Old Testament. Several examples will be cited later in this chapter. For a fuller list and discussion, see Michael Brown, *Answering Jewish Objections to Jesus, vol. 3: Messianic Prophecy Objections* (Baker, 2003).

2. Norman Geisler and William Nix, *A General Introduction to the Bible* (Chicago: Moody, 1986), 176–177.

3. An excellent way to get started reading the Bible is with the *Choosing Your Faith New Testament* (Tyndale, 2008), which includes the full text of the New Testament and explanatory notes by Mark Mittelberg. For more information, see the promotional page in the back of this book.

4. The biblical canon is the collection of authoritative writings comprised in the Bible—the writings that passed the test and proved to have the credentials to be considered part of God's revelation.

5. *The Gnostic Bible*, ed. Willis Barnstone and Marvin Meyer (Boston: Shambhala, 2003), 46, 48, 69, as cited by Lee Strobel in *The Case for the Real Jesus* (Grand Rapids, MI: Zondervan, 2007), 27.

6. 1 John 1:1, NIV

7. Luke 1:1-4

8. John A. T. Robinson, *Redating the New Testament* (Eugene, OR: Wipf & Stock, 2000). Originally published in 1977 by Westminster Press, Philadelphia.

9. People do try to rewrite history, of course—there are some who deny the Jewish Holocaust and others who try to persuade us that President Kennedy and Elvis Presley are really still alive and living on an island somewhere—but their foolishness is evident to any serious observer.

10. For details on outside historical confirmation for Jesus and the early church, see Gary Habermas, *The Historical Jesus: Ancient Evidence for the Life of Christ* (College Press, 1996). See also Josh McDowell and Bill Wilson, *He Walked Among Us: Evidence for the Historical Jesus* (Thomas Nelson, 1993).

11. I once took a tour of a Hindu temple and was candidly told by the official Hindu tour guide, "Our religion is so old we don't even know where it comes from."

12. If you're concerned about the differences in the translations, visit a Christian bookstore and read the same passages from several different versions (or view them online at a site such as www.biblegateway.com). You'll see that they use a variety of English words to get at the same meaning. The differences can actually help you better understand the original message, which is why publishers also produce "interlinear" versions, which put four, six, or sometimes even eight different translations in columns next to each other. One caution, however: The New World Translation, produced by the Watchtower Society of the Jehovah's Witnesses, is not a reliable translation, nor is it supported by reputable biblical scholars. It is contradicted at numerous key points by every reliable version, including the New Living Translation, the New International Version, the New American Standard Bible, the classic King James Version, and many others.

13. For a detailed discussion of the New Testament manuscripts, see chapter 3, "The Documentary Evidence," in Lee Strobel, *The Case for Christ* (Zondervan, 1998).

14. Strobel, *Case for Christ*, 60–61.

15. F. F. Bruce, *The New Testament Documents: Are They Reliable?* 6th ed. (Grand Rapids, MI: Eerdmans, 1981), 11.

16. John Ankerberg said this during the taping of his program, *The John Ankerberg Show*, with guest Lee Strobel in the fall of 2007 (to be aired later). This was relayed to me by Lee Strobel.

17. Frederic G. Kenyon, *The Bible and Archaeology* (New York: Harper and Row, 1940), 288–289.

18. Lee Strobel, *The Case for the Real Jesus* (Grand Rapids, MI: Zondervan, 2007), 83. See also J. Ed Komoszewski, M. James Sawyer, and Daniel B. Wallace, *Reinventing Jesus* (Kregel, 2006).

19. For a great overview of the archeological evidence, see chapter 5, "The Scientific Evidence: Does Archaeology Confirm or Contradict Jesus' Biographies?" in Lee Strobel, *The Case for Christ* (Zondervan, 2003).

20. Sir William Ramsay, *The Bearing of Recent Discovery on the Trustworthiness of the New Testament* (London: Hodder and Stoughton, 1915), 222, as cited in Josh McDowell, *More Than a Carpenter* (Wheaton, IL: Tyndale, 1977), 39.

21. Nelson Glueck, *Rivers in the Desert: A History of the Negev* (New York: Farrar, Straus, and Cudahy, 1959).

22. William F. Albright, "Retrospect and Prospect in New Testament Archaeology," in *The Teacher's Yoke*, E. Jerry Vardaman (Waco, TX: Baylor University Press, 1964), 189, as cited in ed. Norman Geisler and Ron Brooks, *When Skeptics Ask* (Grand Rapids, MI: Baker, 1996), 202.

23. I think Dr. Paul Vitz makes a lot of sense when he describes how some people project their disappointment and frustration with their earthly fathers into the sky and deny the Heavenly Father who actually is there. See Paul Vitz, *Faith of the Fatherless: The Psychology of Atheism* (Spence, 2000).

24. Proverbs 27:6, KJV

25. Isaiah 53:6

26. Lee Strobel, *The Case for Christ: The Film* (Lionsgate Home Entertainment, 2007)

27. Isaiah 53:5

28. Matthew 27:46, NIV

29. Psalm 22:1, 7-8, 14-18, NIV

30. This quote is from Louis Lapides, a Jewish man who was convinced by the evidence of prophecy many years ago to trust in Jesus as his Messiah. He is now the pastor of a church. His story, and this quote, can be found in Lee Strobel, *The Case for Christ* (Zondervan, 1998), 183.

31. If you want to know the odds of *forty-eight* messianic prophecies being fulfilled by one person, see Lee Strobel, *The Case for Christ* (Zondervan, 1998), 183.

32. Luke 24:25-26

33. Luke 24:32

Chapter 11—"How Can I *Figure Out* What to Believe?"

1. John 8:46

2. Abdullah Yusuf Ali, *The Holy Qur-an: text, translation, and commentary* (Lahore, Pakistan: Shaikh Muhammad Ashraf, 1938), Surah 40:55. Emphasis added.

3. For clarity, in keeping with the way that days were counted in that culture, *parts* of three days would be referred to simply as "three days." Jesus was crucified on Good Friday, so he was dead and in the grave for the latter part of Friday, all day Saturday, and the very early part of Sunday, prior to his resurrection. In their way of counting, that was three days.

4. Gary Habermas and Mike Licona, *The Case for the Resurrection of Jesus* (Grand Rapids, MI: Kregel, 2004), 108–109.

5. John 20:28

6. Acts 2:22-24, 32-36

7. Acts 2:38

8. According to the statistics at www.adherents.com, there are currently about 2.2 billion Christians, and almost 1.8 billion Muslims.

9. Acts 26:26

10. See Acts 6:8–8:1.

11. Acts 8:1, 9:1

12. The account of Saul's (Paul's) conversion is in Acts 9.

13. Simon Greenleaf, *The Testimony of the Evangelists: The Gospels Examined by the Rules of Evidence* (Grand Rapids, MI: Kregel Classics, 1995), 8. Originally published in 1874.

14. Ibid.

15. Sir Lionel Luckhoo, "The Question Answered." This article can be found online at www.hawaiichristiansonline.com/sir_lionel.html. Select the link for "The Question Answered" booklet. The quote appears on the last page of the article.

16. Josh McDowell, *More Than a Carpenter* (Carol Stream, IL: Tyndale, 2004), and *Evidence That Demands a Verdict* (San Bernardino, Calif.: Here's Life, 1979). An updated edition of *Evidence That Demands a Verdict* was published by Authentic Lifestyle in 2004.

17. Viggo Olsen published his story in a booklet titled "The Agnostic Who Dared to Search," (Chicago: Moody Press, 1974). He also published stories of his time in Bangladesh, in *Daktar: Diplomat in Bangladesh* (Moody Press, 1973), and *Daktar II* (Moody Press, 1990).

18. John 14:6

19. John 8:32

20. Matthew 11:28-30

21. Greenleaf, *Testimony of the Evangelists*, 11.

Chapter 12—"I'd *Like* to Have Faith"

1. My calculations are based on statistics given at www.unitedjustice.com/death-statistics.html and at http://users.frii.com/mytymyk/lions/intro.htm.

2. Richard Dawkins, during a lecture at the 1992 Edinburgh International Science Festival, as cited by Alister McGrath, in *Dawkins' God: Genes, Memes, and the Meaning of Life* (Malden, MA: Blackwell, 2004), 84.

3. I'm aware that the phrase I'm using, *reasonable faith*, is also the title of a book by William Lane Craig (Crossway, 1994) and the name of the organization he runs (www.reasonablefaith.org)—and I recommend both of them!

4. Luke 6:46

5. Matthew 20:28

6. Rudolf Bultmann, *New Testament and Mythology and Other Basic Writings* (Minneapolis, MN: Fortress, 1984).

7. See 2 Peter 3:9-10, which says, "The Lord isn't really being slow about his promise, as some people think. No, he is being patient for your sake. He does not want anyone to be destroyed, but wants everyone to repent. But the day of the Lord will come as unexpectedly as a thief." Also see verse 15 in that same chapter.

8. John 16:33 (the first half)

9. John 16:33 (the second half)

10. Hebrews 4:15-16

11. C. S. Lewis, *Mere Christianity* (New York: Macmillan, 1960), 45.

12. Ibid., 45–46. Emphasis his.

13. For answers to 800 of these kinds of challenges and issues related to the Bible, I recommend Norman Geisler and Thomas Howe, *When Skeptics Ask: A Popular Handbook on Bible Difficulties* (Victor, 1992). Also see Gleason L. Archer, Jr., *New International Encyclopedia of Bible Difficulties* (Zondervan, 2001).

14. To find a great list of generally relevant and accessible churches, visit www. willowcreek.com and click on "Find a Church." If you hit "Map It," you can search by city, state, or zip code. Also, to find the kinds of discussion groups I mentioned, check with the churches you find on that database, or look for something in your area called Alpha Groups, which have helped people in their spiritual journeys all over the world, by clicking on www.alphana.org (Alpha North America). Also, if you're interested in starting this kind of a group yourself, you should read Garry Poole's helpful book, *Seeker Small Groups: Engaging Spiritual Seekers in Life-Changing Discussions* (Zondervan, 2003).

15. Aldous Huxley, *Ends and Means* (London: Chatto & Windus, 1969), 270, 273. Emphasis added.

16. See, for example, Luke 6:41-42 and all of Matthew 23.

17. Matthew 11:28

18. Friedrich Nietzsche, *The Antichrist*, trans. Anthony Ludovici (Amherst, NY: Prometheus, 2000), 72. Originally published in 1895.

19. Have you seen the T-shirts that are out there? On one side it says, "'God is dead,' signed Nietzsche." On the other side it says, "'Nietzsche is dead,' signed God."

20. Lewis, *Mere Christianity*, 108–109, 111.

21. John 8:32

22. Matthew 13:46 (KJV) says, "When he had found one pearl of great price, [he] went and sold all that he had, and bought it."

23. John 10:10, NIV

24. "No One Believes in Me Anymore," words and music by Keith Green and Melody Green. Copyright © 1978 April Music. All rights reserved.

25. James 4:7-10. Emphasis added.

26. John 10:9-10

27. John 3:16-18

28. Luke 19:10

29. From Jesus' words, describing himself, in John 14:6

30. Romans 10:13

Chapter 13—The *Benefits* of Choosing Your Faith Wisely

1. "The Wall," by Kerry Livgren. Copyright © 1976 Don Kirshner Music (BMI). Used by permission. All rights reserved.

2. Steve Jobs, speaking for the 2005 commencement at Stanford University, June 12, 2005. The transcript can be found online at http://news-service.stanford.edu/news/2005/june15/jobs-061505.html.

3. Jesus, in Revelation 3:20

FOR FURTHER READING

Choosing Your Faith New Testament, with notes by Mark Mittelberg (Tyndale, 2008)

The Case for Christ by Lee Strobel (Zondervan, 1998)

The Case for Faith by Lee Strobel (Zondervan, 2000)

The Case for a Creator by Lee Strobel (Zondervan, 2004)

The Case for the Real Jesus by Lee Strobel (Zondervan, 2007)

More Than a Carpenter by Josh McDowell (Tyndale, 1977)

Know Why You Believe by Paul Little (InterVarsity, 1970)

Mere Christianity by C. S. Lewis (Macmillan, 1952)

The Purpose Driven Life by Rick Warren (Zondervan, 2002)

Jesus Among Other Gods by Ravi Zacharias (W, 2000)

Putting Jesus in His Place by Robert Bowman and J. Ed Komoszewski (Kregel, 2007)

Mormonism 101 by Bill McKeever and Eric Johnson (Baker, 2000)

Reasonable Faith by William Lane Craig (Crossway, 2004)

Building Belief by Chad V. Meister (Baker, 2006)

I Don't Have Enough Faith to Be an Atheist by Norman Geisler and Frank Turek (Crossway, 2004)

FOR ONLINE RESEARCH

www.LeeStrobel.com — features video clips on a variety of faith questions and issues

www.ReasonableFaith.org — site of William Lane Craig, a great philosopher of religion

www.JesusCentral.com — primary source for information about the Jesus of history

www.Metamorpha.com — discussions on spiritual formation and development

www.WillowCreek.com — click "Find a Church" for relevant places to explore faith

And visit us at www.ChoosingYourFaith.com

ABOUT THE AUTHOR

Mark Mittelberg is a best-selling author, a sought-after speaker, and a leading strategist in outreach and apologetics. He is the author of *Becoming a Contagious Church;* coauthor with Bill Hybels of the best-selling book *Becoming a Contagious Christian;* and a contributing editor to *The Journey: A Bible for the Spiritually Curious.* He is also the primary author of the celebrated *Becoming a Contagious Christian* training course, which has been translated into twenty languages and taught to more than a million people around the world.

Mark was the outreach director for Willow Creek Community Church and the Willow Creek Association for more than a decade. He was an editorial consultant and a periodic guest for Lee Strobel's weekly television show, *Faith Under Fire.* He is a contributing editor for *Outreach* magazine, and a regular speaker for the Church Communication Network satellite broadcasts to sites across North America. Mark has a master's degree in philosophy of religion from Trinity Evangelical Divinity School. He lives in Southern California with his wife, Heidi, and their two children.

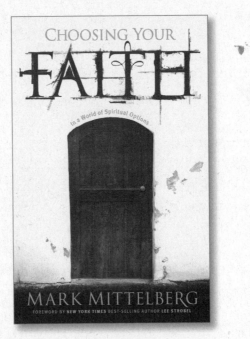